Simpsons
the cook book

To TREVOR

"HAPPY COOKING"

Adam

Quail

22/6

By Andreas Antona
with Adam Bennett & Luke Tipping

Foreword by Brian Turner CBE

Andreas Antona is a loveable man, his character and his always smiling face help portray his desire to get people round a table, eating, drinking and laughing. To me he is a great friend and a fabulous host. Every time I meet him either in his restaurant, the fabulous Simpsons, or in someone else's restaurant I am sure to be there for ages, not wanting to leave for fear of missing some gastronomic or alcoholic delight.

Andreas is a team leader by nature, a family man and this shows both front and back of house in his restaurant, and at University College Birmingham, where he is on the board of governors.

Everyone who has worked with Andreas speaks so lovingly of the way he teaches his skills learnt over the years, from his childhood days with his family to great hotels like The Ritz and The Dorchester or to Zurich, Germany and then back to Birmingham.

Birmingham has now a reputation for fine dining and good eating like it never had; this is largely due to Andreas and his determination to feed his guests good, honest, classic food and his desire to pass on his experience and knowledge to the next generations.

Andreas is a formidable part of the 'Brum Mafia' ... I know who they are, they know who they are and together they intend to see that Birmingham continues to grow in stature and reputation as middle England's centre of gastronomy.

Brian Turner CBE

Dedications

This book is dedicated to my wife Alison and our children Laura, Michael, Lisa and Sofia.

I have been a very fortunate and lucky man to achieve my ambitions but like all good things in life you need support. I have found this over many, many years through my wife. Like my children, she is a constant source of inspiration.

Acknowledgements

It's a daunting task to acknowledge everyone who has been involved in a production like this. So whether I mention you by name or by association... thank you – I couldn't have done it without you.

Firstly, I would like to thank Luke Tipping and my co-author Adam Bennett, for their valuable insight and dedication to the running of Simpsons.

There are many other people in our brigade both front and back of house who work tirelessly for the cause and to fly the flag not only for Simpsons but British gastronomy. To mention just a few, Matt Cheal and Simon Morris, true diamonds who have worked with me for more than ten years... Jacqueline Keenan for her fine chocolate skills, Kristian Curtis for his natural ability in baking bread and in particular Tony Selimaj and Fanny Papelierm, part of our great front of house team.

We must also not forget Sue Byrane, our administrator, who keeps us all in check and in good shape to face our daily tasks.

I would also like to thank Jodi Hinds for her professionalism and great photographs and all the team at RMC, in particular Martin Edwards and Paul Cocker.

This, my second book, came about really by the encouragement of my dear friend Brian Turner who has kindly written the foreword for which I thank him also.

Written by: Andreas Antona with
Adam Bennett and Luke Tipping at:
Simpsons Restaurant
20 Highfield Road
Edgbaston,
Birmingham B15 3DU
Telephone (0121) 454 3434
www.simpsonsrestaurant.co.uk

Edited by:

Martin Edwards, Chris Brierley
RMC Books – (0114) 250 6300

Design by:

Paul Cocker
RMC Books – (0114) 250 6300

Photography by:

Jodi Hinds – www.jodihinds.com

Contributors:

Karen Horsefield, Victoria Philpott

First Published in 2011 on behalf of:
Simpsons Restaurant
www.simpsonsrestaurant.co.uk

Published by:
RMC Books – www.rmcbooks.co.uk

Contents

Starters

Main Courses

Desserts

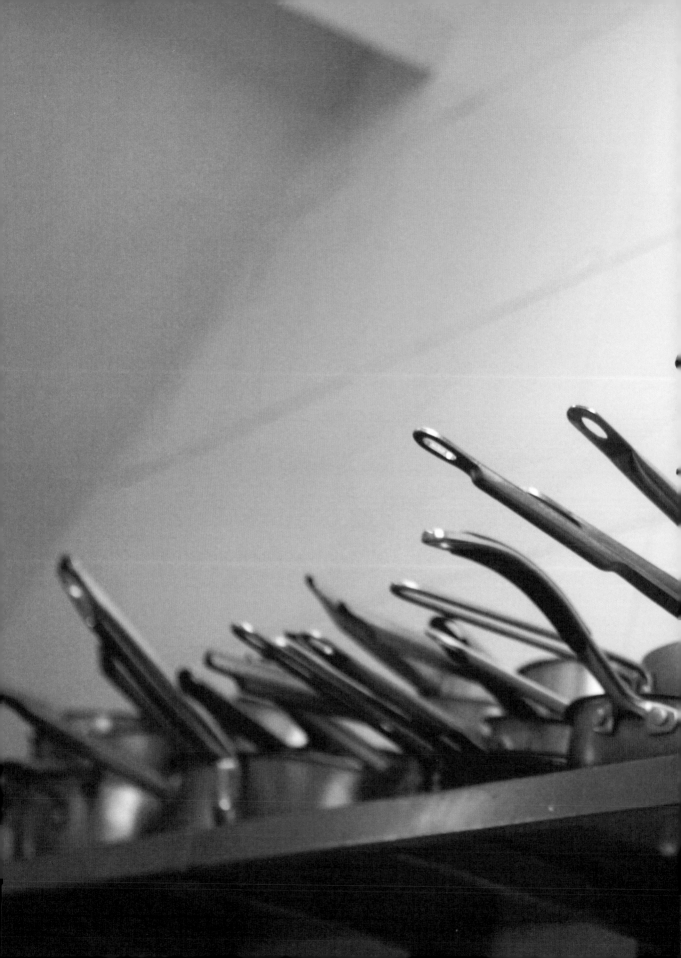

Introduction

I grew up amongst the smells and sounds of a busy kitchen. My father, a Greek Cypriot, ran a restaurant in the West End and my uncle owned a specialist deli. My aunts and uncles grew exotic vegetables in the garden and my palate was constantly bombarded with exciting tastes. In the early days we lived above the kitchen and it was impossible to escape from the bustle of cooking and service. Luckily, it was an atmosphere I relished and I had no problem leaving behind my homework when I was called downstairs to wash plates or chop vegetables. To my father it was more important that I bonded with the family and developed a work ethic than bother with schoolwork. Cooking intoxicated me and I knew from a very young age that this was what I wanted to do.

Much of the cooking done at home was rustic with strong Greek influences, but at the time the leading force in culinary matters was France and that was the schooling you received as a young chef. I have still great regard for French cuisine and their attitude to eating. I learned a lot when I made a gastronomic visit to Lyon in the 80s and saw restaurateurs buying fresh herbs and vegetables at market from men turning up with heavily-laden pushbikes. Not only did they have an abundance of fabulous fresh produce, they also had respect for it. I was captivated by the power of tradition in this country where restaurant owners laid down wine in cellars for their children alongside bottles their own fathers had bought for them. Despite this, I think the French mantle has fallen away and the best chefs in Europe are now British. We have plenty of raw talent and a more educated and demanding public to satisfy. We just need to channel our expertise in the right way. For that reason, I'm not a fan of fads. I think dishes should be ageless and we shouldn't sacrifice tradition at the altar of fashion. In our kitchens we like to keep things simple. Our cooking techniques are largely basic and allow the flavours of the food to speak for themselves, with a little enhancement. That's harder to achieve than it sounds. Precision, care and attention are our watchwords. Take, for example, a good piece of beef. It takes 18 months to rear, four weeks to hang and 10 minutes to f*** it up if you don't cook it correctly.

I love mistakes. It's one of the few ways we learn.

Cooking takes patience, practice and passion. I had plenty of practice as a child and already had passion. When I started a cookery course at Ealing College, I impressed fellow students with my adept knife drill and the way I could toss baking beans in a pan blindfold. I already had the skills they were yet to learn, something I could thank my father for. Some of the skills I take for granted like chopping onions quickly or cracking an egg one-handed fascinate other people, but we chefs take them for granted. We live and breathe cooking and our methods and techniques come quite naturally to us. But for others, it takes time to build confidence and this book will focus on helping pass some of our skills to you. Back to my early career, I still had a lot to learn; college taught me discipline and made me focus on haute cuisine. After qualifying I knew I had to leave London to expand my knowledge and I set off for Zurich, working in a restaurant in the station and then to Germany to cook at the International Stuttgart Hotel. On my rare days off I visited a variety of restaurants, trying out both haute cuisine and rustic styles of cooking. I learned as much from those field trips as I did in my own kitchens. I still eat out regularly and get plenty of ideas on what works and what doesn't. It helps me keep the customer's point of view alive.

The person who attracted me back to London was the rising young star Anton Mosimann, a Swiss chef whose fresh style of cooking was breathing new life into the British culinary scene. In the 1980s Mosimann was king of the kitchen at the Dorchester and one of the first-ever celebrity chefs, commanding a huge following thanks to his cookbooks and TV shows. Many of the chefs he trained went on to win Michelin stars after leaving to set up on their own. Fortunately I was one of his boys and his influence left an indelible mark on my approach to cooking. I moved from his kitchen to work for Michael Quinn – or the Mighty Quinn as he was then known. Quinn had been headhunted to fill the post of head chef at the Ritz. As a young man and the first British head chef in the hotel's 74-year history, it was his remit to reinvigorate the restaurant's tired format, which he did in style. I was part of that revolution and our fantastic success gave me the confidence and competence to start my own place.

Together with my wife Alison, a second commis chef at The Ritz, we opened the doors of Simpsons in Kenilworth in 1993. Why Simpsons? It was the name of the chemist shop we had taken over and we decided to keep it. We served a variety of food influenced by my days at the Ritz and Dorchester, together with rustic cooking from my childhood, including Kleftiko (braised shank of lamb, which is still on the menu today). Simpsons was an instant success and won a Michelin star in 1999. We moved in 2004 to our present home, a stunning Georgian grade II listed mansion with gardens in leafy Edgbaston. The location suited me perfectly. I've always had a soft spot for grand,

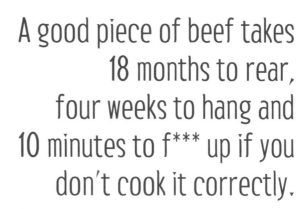

> A good piece of beef takes
> 18 months to rear,
> four weeks to hang and
> 10 minutes to f*** up if you
> don't cook it correctly.

iconic restaurants and the relaxed country house style we've evoked here complements our food and hospitality. I knew when we set up I wanted to create a venue with an air of longevity: the feeling of Chippendale, not flat-packed furniture. We've worked hard to keep the standards high and preserve our Michelin star because we know you're only as good as your last meal. I have a hardworking team front of house and in the kitchen who make sure our customers are contented from the moment they walk in until they leave.

Of course the star of the show will always be the food and the creation of quality meals relies on the finest ingredients. Freshness is always a key prerequisite so where possible I buy locally and have developed links with local farmers to set up a reliable supply of meat and vegetables. However, I'm not a slave to buying locally and if I can get better produce elsewhere, I will. We're regularly supplied from the immense Rungis market in Paris – it's the largest market in the world and unsurpassed in terms of the variety and excellence of food on offer. The essential thing is to never compromise on quality. Find a good butcher and greengrocer and you can be confident of your raw ingredients. My other advice about cooking is to not be afraid of making mistakes. I love mistakes – it's one of the few ways we learn. It's also important to develop a curiosity about how flavours work together and keep cooking. At Simpsons we don't all sit down and make up a new menu every day of the week. Our repertoire has gradually evolved over time. We tinker, change, experiment and come up with different ways of cooking a dish.

One of the greatest pleasures of my career has been to see fledgling cooks go on to become fine chefs, sometimes with their own kitchens. It is a privilege to pass on skills to others, something we also do through our cookery school. We hope this book will help you develop your own cooking. The recipes will open up new worlds of flavour, encourage you to try something different and give you some useful tips along the way. Enjoy!

Andreas

Adam Bennett, Luke Tipping and the team

This book aims to demystify how to make fantastic food, from the first step of selecting the best raw ingredients and cooking them accurately, to presenting the dish beautifully on the plate. We've spent many hours trawling through menus from Simpsons to find the most inspirational recipes that will work for you. We've only included dishes that really jumped off the page at us. Every recipe in this book is worth the effort of shopping and cooking.

People often ask us how we get ideas for recipes, a question with many answers. Some flavour combinations suggest themselves while we're cooking. We may have a brainwave and try something out, however wacky it might seem and then get feedback from staff (our favourite guinea pigs). Foie gras and banana made some people raise their eyebrows, but it really worked. We also get ideas when eating out ourselves, either in the UK or abroad. Most frequently we take inspiration from produce in season. Our veg supplier at Rungis may tell us there are some lovely broad bean flowers, golden beetroot or a rare variety of pepper available. Those ingredients act as muse for a new dish or to add a twist to an old one.

Whatever we cook, we try to build a balanced mixture of tones and textures that still allows each element to preserve its pristine flavour. For that reason, we favour simplicity; we don't like to distort the clean flavour of our fresh ingredients. It's a myth that impressive cooking has to be complicated.

While we love creating novel dishes, we never slavishly follow fashion in the food world. We've been around long enough to see through most crazes, so we take what we want from them and move on. Quality cuisine doesn't spring up overnight; it takes years to develop and perfect. We've found that what works is evolution, not revolution. Fusion food, molecular gastronomy and tapas style presentation have all been in vogue at various times. If we ever borrow from fashion, we do so with a very light touch – a slight nod in that direction, rather than a full embrace.

As chefs we may represent the glamorous side of the kitchen, but we treat every job with the same respect, from prepping to washing up, often working alongside our colleagues. By mucking in, we get to recognise individuals with potential or particular talents and encourage them in the right direction.

Home chefs can learn a lot from the way a restaurant kitchen works. We know the best ways to save you time and expense, whether by prudent shopping or preparing things in advance. We hope this book gives you plenty of ideas to enthuse you and build your culinary skills and confidence. If your preparation is good and your cooking is accurate, you're guaranteed some wonderful results.

The Welcome

When I give staff training on hospitality, I ask them this simple question: what would you do if I turned up at your house at 8am one morning? Answers range from 'open the door' to 'offer you a drink'. Sometimes it takes a while to get the response I'm after which is to smile. It sounds simple, but showing you're pleased to see people, even if it's a little early in the day, is the most important part of making them feel welcome.

At Simpsons we like to make our guests feel comfortable about being there from the very outset. I come from a Greek background, where greeting people can be very demonstrative and warm hugs and kisses are freely exchanged. Traditionally, guests were offered jam, glace fruits and cold water after they'd escaped your embraces. That ritualistic hospitality has disappeared from Greek households nowadays, but the sentiment is still there. Elsewhere in the world, a variety of etiquettes have dictated the way visitors are welcomed over the centuries, some of them rather bizarre. While Egyptian hosts would anoint guests with oil, Arabs would pour melted butter on their heads. Both options were probably preferable to how a lowly guest was greeted in Java; he'd be offered his host's half-chewed betel nut as a form of compliment.

What every culture has in common is the practice of offering sustenance to guests. Sharing food is a marker of kinship that prevails to the present day, although hosts no longer tend to drink or eat first to assure guests nothing is poisoned.

We at Simpsons concentrate on putting our guests at ease and making sure they have everything they need to feel at home. I think hospitality is about showing people the goodness within your heart. But the art of hospitality doesn't come easily to everyone, which is why we spend a lot of time training our front of house staff. This often involves sending them to work with masters of their trade at distinguished restaurants in Europe. They come back inspired, determined to develop into better professionals.

Our front of house team is a vital part of our restaurant, which is why we wanted to salute them in this book. The cooking is only ever one part of the whole.

Simpsons People

People arrive at Michelin-starred restaurants with preconceptions. They imagine the service will be arrogant and stuffy and the staff will be walking around with brooms up their backs. They are in for a surprise if so.

We greet our guests and take them to the salon for an aperitif whilst they peruse the menu. This is a really important time for me as we can work out what kind of mood they are in so we can tailor our service accordingly. The chefs de range (headwaiters) are made aware of anything relevant about our guests.

It might sound odd, but this job involves a lot of psychology as well as good communication skills. We need to be attuned to our customers and sense whether they are having a good time or not. Our staff are so well-attuned to the mood of the diners that they can tell by sweeping their eyes over the room whether someone is unhappy or waiting too long for something. Their job is to rectify these problems immediately.

In France, working in a restaurant is a respected career. Here in England the profession has been rather looked down on for years. I've been around long enough to see that view has gradually changed. The public has become more discerning and demanding. Guests are right to have a high level of expectation about their entire dining experience. We try to fulfil that at Simpsons, which is why the quality of our service is as important as the cooking.

Andreas

Love Your Dough

The alchemy of bread making is what makes it so appealing. It's one of the reasons it has held a place in every cuisine throughout the world for over 5,000 years. Bread is one of the oldest prepared foods in the world and a dietary staple. No wonder we have become a little blasé about picking a loaf off the shelf in a supermarket without a second thought. But there is much more to bread than white sliced, as any good baker knows.

Basic bread making is a craft that has been largely lost to this generation – whereas making daily bread was a routine chore for thousands of years. Now with the convenience of bought bread or the hassle-free solution of bread making machines, we've lost touch with kneading, proving and baking process.

At Simpson's, we still make bread in the traditional way. Fresh bread rolls and loaves are prepared each day for our diners. In addition to the familiar white rolls and sour dough loaves, we like to create different breads with a twist, often reflecting the seasons. In spring, we make breads such as wild garlic and goat's cheese, or a focaccia style of bread with air-dried cherry tomatoes, goat's cheese and fennel seed. Another popular combination is dry-fried cumin seeds and Gruyere cheese. The possibilities are endless – there are so many different types of doughs and a multitude of ingredients that can be added to transform this once basic food from the delicious to the sublime.

The Heart of a Breadmaker

B read exemplifies what we strive to do at Simpsons – to take good plain ingredients and to turn them into something special. Flour, water, yeast, salt... it doesn't sound much by itself. But add that vital element, the breadmaker's craft, and the result can be as intriguing, as varied and as irresistible as anything else that the kitchen produces.

"I began working at Simpsons preparing vegetables but when the opportunity arose to learn the art of bread, I seized it. I didn't think it would be too interesting at first, but I quickly became obsessed with bread. I love trying out different recipes and I find the whole process of kneading and shaping dough quite therapeutic!

Achieving consistency is a crucial part of what I do. Each batch of rolls has to be like the one before it and this can be tricky to achieve when for example the weather becomes hot and dough rises too quickly. Then I have to keep adding ice to the water to ensure a controlled proving process.

Sourdough bread is a favourite of mine, it's the most natural way to make bread as it uses airborne yeasts which we cultivate in our sourdough starter or "mother." This means that our sourdough is unique to the Edgbaston microclimate as the combinations of wild yeasts vary from place to place.

While I strive to keep consistency, I also enjoy experimenting with different flavours, not always successfully. My first attempt with seaweed butter produced the worst bread in the world. Needless to say, that disaster stayed in the kitchen, but I finally perfected the recipe.

If you're new to bread baking, start with a basic recipe for white or brown rolls before you begin to add anything exciting. Once you're confident you've mastered that, the sky's the limit."

Christian

White Bread Rolls

Ingredients

500g strong white flour
20g fresh yeast
12g salt
275ml water at room temperature
50g old dough, optional (from yesterday's bread)

Method

1. Combine all the ingredients to form a dough and work for 10 minutes by hand or 6-8 minutes on a machine. Contine until the dough is shiny and elastic.
2. Cover the dough and leave at room temperature until it doubles in size.
3. Turn the dough out onto your worktop and cut into 30g pieces.
4. Mould each one into mini baguette shapes, dust lightly with flour and slash each 3 times with a sharp knife.
5. Cover loosely with cling film and leave to prove in a warm place until doubled in size.
6. Bake at 220ºC, with a tray of hot water on the oven base, for about 5 minutes. Then carefully remove the water and bake for a further 4-5 minutes until golden.
7. Check the rolls by tapping the bottom – they should sound hollow.
8. Cool the rolls on a wire rack.

Tapenade Bread

Method

1. Mix all the ingredients together except the second 100g of butter, which will be folded in later.
2. When the dough has come together and is smooth, cover the bowl with cling film and chill the dough for around 3 hours.
3. Ensure the remaining butter is at room temperature and a spreadable consistency.
4. Roll the chilled dough to create a rectangle of about 1cm thickness.
5. Spread the butter over two-thirds of the rectangle, leaving one third free with a 1cm gap at the edge.
6. Fold the unbuttered third over onto the middle third, then the other buttered third on top.
7. Roll the layered dough out again to a thickness of 1cm and repeat the folding process. Repeat this process once more then place the dough onto a tray and cover with cling film.
8. Chill the dough for a minimum of 3 hours or up to 12 hours.
9. Roll the well-chilled dough 3mm thick to a rectangle about 20cm across.
10. Spread with tapenade, leaving a 1cm border at the top edge of the strip.
11. Brush this border with water. Start to roll the dough from the edge nearest to you so that the wet border will seal the whole roll.
12. Cut the roll into pieces of about 40g.
13. Place each piece into greased pastry rings (7cm tall & 7cm diameter) on an oven tray.
14. Move to a warm place until the dough has almost reached the top of the ring.
15. Bake in a hot oven (225°C) for 8-10 minutes, until golden and crisp.
16. Remove from the rings and cool on a wire rack.

Ingredients

500g strong bread flour
25g fresh yeast
12g salt
10g sugar
100g butter
365ml milk
100g butter at room temperature, for folding
4 tbsp black olive tapenade

99% - A taste of chocolate

by Jacqueline (Chocolate) Keenan

You may think we're obsessed with the stuff, but we've got nothing on the ancient tribes who first cultivated chocolate. The Aztecs, Mayans and Incas worshipped chocolate and used cocoa beans as currency (ten beans bought a rabbit, a hundred bought a slave). They even buried people with cocoa pods and drawings of chocolate. They enjoyed it as a spicy, frothy drink and thought it would imbue the drinker with superpowers. In some respects they were right.

A moderate amount of dark chocolate is good for you. It actually boasts eight times as many antioxidants as strawberries as well as iron, sodium, potassium and other essential nutrients. And it's rather more palatable than a multivitamin pill.

Until the 16th century chocolate was unknown in Europe, when it was brought back from Mexico to Spain and prized by the nobility as a sweetened drink. It wasn't until the 1800s that a process for making bars of chocolate was perfected and only recently that chocolate ceased to be a luxurious treat for the lucky few.

Chocolate starts life in melon-shaped cocoa pods grown on Theobroma trees only in regions 20 degrees north and south of the equator. Each pod carries between 20 and 50 beans, which are harvested, fermented, roasted, sorted, crushed, liquified and finally tempered. The whole business of manufacture is complicated and lengthy – no wonder it took so many years to perfect.

The taste of a particular chocolate depends on what strain of tree it is from, where it is grown and how it is blended – a little like grapes and wine. At Simpsons, we use different types of chocolate from Venezuela, Madagascar, Peru and Ghana, each with their own distinctive flavour, naturally suited to specific uses or taste combinations.

So there's a great deal of science involved in chocolate, and there's a lot to learn. That's why I found myself on a special training course devoted entirely to the subject.

As training courses go, it was the pick of the bunch. Some people might even call it their dream ticket. It's true spending time surrounded by chocolate is a pleasant way to learn. But there's a serious purpose behind it all. I completed my chocolate training at the world-renowned Valrhona Ecole du grand chocolat in France, where supreme quality is the byword and the skills taught in the kitchen are second to none. Great chocolate delivers its pure taste like a hit: there's no flavour-masking fat coating your palate. We use chocolate with high cocoa solids, which guarantees the taste. Even our milk chocolate has 40% cocoa, which is more that in your average plain chocolate bar."

My favourite is probably Valrhona's Manjari from Madagascar. A clean, acidic dark chocolate, with a bouquet of red fruits, lending itself to Alphonso mangos, raspberries and pastries. Caraibe, made exclusively from the prized Caribbean grown Trinitario bean, is rounded with warm roasted coffee, fruit and nut notes, the perfect partner for chestnuts and other nuts. Guanaja, from the eponymous Caribbean island, has a powerful taste with floral notes. I use this for chocolate soufflés, cakes, ganaches and petit fours.

Araguani from Venezuela has an intense flavour thanks to its high percentage of cocoa solids. It has warm notes of liquorice, raisin and chestnuts. Nyangbo, made solely from beans grown in Ghana, has a mild smoothness, spiked with sweet spices.

I learned how to temper chocolate on the Valrhona course, which has opened up a world of possibilities, allowing me to add different flavours and achieve a variety of textures. The course was important in another way. It was here I met Adam, one of the head chefs at Simpsons, who led me to my job at the restaurant.

I'm lucky that the kitchen here is incredibly creative and I'm given free rein to experiment with new ways of creating chocolate and chocolate-based desserts, the more challenging the better. Recently I mastered the art of making marble chocolates using a range of brightly coloured cocoa butters for the shell that I filled with ganache. I teach customers to make these pretty creations on the popular chocolate courses we run at the restaurant.

People are incredibly excited when they turn out chocolates they have crafted themselves. I still get the same thrill every time I produce a tray myself. Chocolate making is a mixture of science, art and craft. I'm in total agreement with the Aztecs: chocolate is utterly divine.

Jacqueline

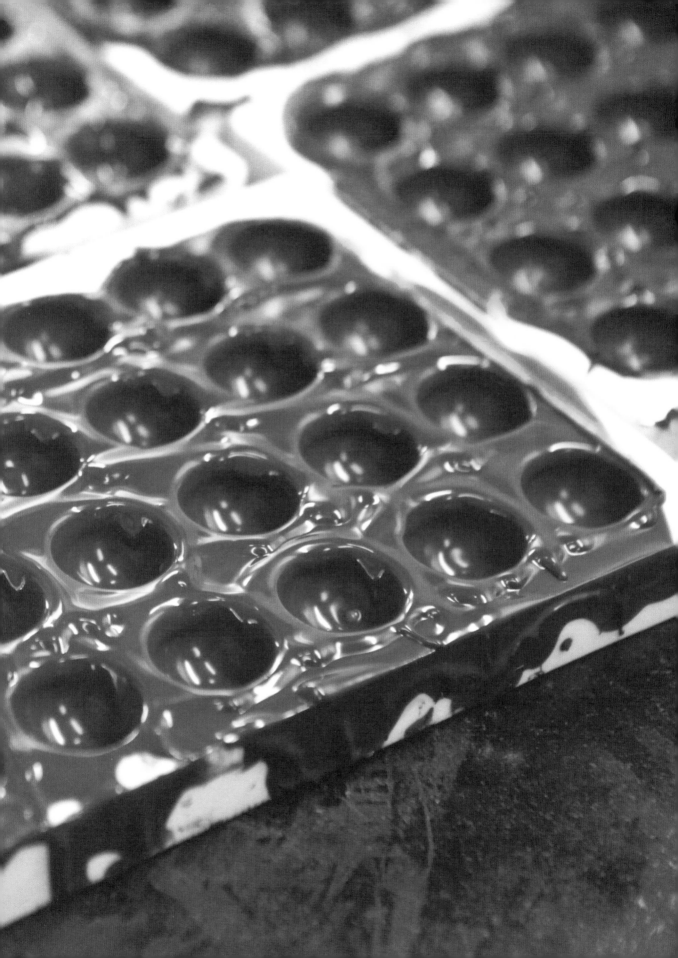

Rungis Market – Our Local

Never let it be said that chefs don't care about customer satisfaction. Take the case of the French chef Francois Vatel. He'd already made something of a name for himself as one of the nation's best, and his crowning glory came when, in 1671, he was chosen to prepare a banquet for Louis XIV, the Sun King, and 200 of his entourage. It was no mean task, and Vatel gave it his all. It left him sleep-deprived and exhausted. Tempers flared in the kitchen. But worse was to come.

He was pushed over the edge when his fish order arrived seriously short. His honour at stake, there was only one thing to do. He ran himself through with a ceremonial sword. The banquet proceeded, minus the fish course, in deference to the late chef. But all ended happily. The missing fish was delivered some time later. Now although I expect total commitment from my chefs, I draw the line at this kind of conduct. It makes an awful mess of the kitchen.

The story does however underline two things. First, the French take their food very seriously. And secondly, reliable suppliers are utterly crucial to a good operation. Get a good supplier and you have the makings of a fabulous menu.

At Simpsons, we rely on some excellent British growers and farmers for fine, seasonal produce, but we also follow the example of our cross-Channel cousins and use the market nicknamed 'the Stomach of France'.

Rungis Market is renowned as the largest and best supplier of fresh produce in the world. Based in the outskirts of Paris, it commands an area larger than the principality of Monaco, a staggering 232 hectares. With 1.5 million tonnes of food arriving daily from around the globe, it's little wonder the market has its own train station and motorway exit.

My own experience of markets began in London, where my father owned a restaurant. He'd take me to the old Covent Garden, Smithfield, Brentford and Billingsgate two or three times a week. I remember the markets as being magical places, filled with a cast of Dickensian characters and old rogues, bartering and haggling. We'd sit with big mugs of tea and bacon sandwiches, catching up on their gossip and finding out how business was going. Even more than the people, I remember the produce. I loved the way I could touch, smell and taste things to check what was ripe and fresh. I still do the same in supermarkets now; it drives my wife mad! When I first set foot in Rungis, I was awe-struck. It was so much bigger and better than any market I'd ever visited. I still see it as God's hub of excellence. Whatever you want, you can buy there because somewhere in the world certain fruits and vegetables will be in season. I respect the bounty each season brings in our country, but I think too many restaurants are in a stranglehold when they set themselves up to just buy locally. It's not a guarantee of quality and curtails your choice. Besides, we are situated in the middle of a city with few growers nearby.

We chose to expand our options, not limit them, so Rungis market became our favoured supplier. We have a sourcing agent there who stays in regular contact with our chefs, Adam and Luke and consults them whenever we change menus.

I still like to get over to Rungis when I can. It's a cult destination for serious chefs from around the world: nowhere else can you experience the range and quality of produce on offer. While the market is only open to trade customers, dedicated foodies regularly join special tours starting at 5.30am to sample its atmosphere. If you're ever in France, it's worth dragging yourself out of bed for the experience. And don't worry about missing the other sights: from Rungis there's a great view of the Arc de Triomphe and the Eiffel Tower.

Within its vast, covered halls, thousands of sellers begin their day when Parisians are still asleep, trading fruit and vegetables, dairy produce, meat, fish and fresh flowers. Each range of food is displayed in separate covered market sections that open at various times, all ridiculously early. It's quite a feat to get around every supplier, haggling as you go. Some buyers travel by pushbike up and down the endless aisles and many take a break at a market cafe for lunch at around 6am, perhaps accompanied by a glass or two of wine.

Rungis is the backbone of France's fresh food industry and supplies one fifth of the country's population via restaurants, supermarkets and delis. The majority of produce makes its way to neighbouring European buyers or is flown overseas via nearby Orly airport. The food that has been carefully selected for Simpsons is brought by refrigerated van from the market via tunnel or ferry directly to our door in less than 24 hours. No lost sleep, no late fish.

Baked Hen's Egg with Crushed Celeriac, Truffle and Croutons

Serves 4

Method

Note: Even without the truffle this is a sensational combination.

For the garnish

1. Cook the celeriac in simmering, salted water until tender but not waterlogged. Drain well.
2. Crush the hot celeriac with the butter, a pinch of white pepper and any salt to taste. A potato masher is the ideal tool for this but remember to keep some texture in the celeriac. Keep warm until needed.
3. Heat the vegetable oil over a moderate flame and fry the celery leaves until crisp. Drain well on kitchen towel and season with salt.

To finish and serve

Note: The traditional French sur le plat (a sort of saucer with ears) is ideal for this dish. However, a ramekin will work just as well. You will need 4 of your chosen dishes.

1. Place a generous spoonful of warm, crushed celeriac in each dish and make a well in the centre large enough for an egg. Top each egg with a teaspoon each of cream and butter. Place in a preheated oven at 170°C for 8 minutes or so or until the egg is cooked to your preference. Soft yolks are ideal as this becomes the sauce for the dish.
2. When done, serve immediately topped with crispy celery leaves, croutons, Madeira sauce and truffle if required. Top with a pinch of sea salt and a grind of black pepper.

Ingredients

4 large hens eggs, preferably free range

4 tsp butter

4 tsp double cream

Sea salt and black pepper

The leaves from inside a celery heart

100ml vegetable oil

4 dstsp Madeira sauce (see Essential Basics section), optional

1 small truffle, optional

2 tbsp croutons (see blade of beef dish page 115)

For the celeriac

1 small celeriac, peeled and diced

75g butter

Salt and black pepper

This is a sensational combination of textures and flavours, even without the truffle. Creamy celeriac, soft egg yolk and crunchy croutons.

Severn & Wye Smoked Salmon, Portland Crab Meat, Avocado Emulsion, Red Pepper and Sesame Taco

Serves 4

Ingredients

4 slices of smoked salmon, trimmed to long rectangles

200g picked white crab meat

2-3 tbsp mayonnaise

A handful of salad shoots and herbs

1 red pepper

1 tbsp olive oil

1 avocado

4 tsp lemon juice

3 tsp caviar, optional

For the sesame taco

1 egg

1 egg white

70g flour and a pinch of salt

20g warm melted butter

2 tsp white sesame seeds

2 tsp black sesame seeds

A pinch of Maldon salt flakes

Method

For the tacos

1. Whisk the yolk and whole egg together briefly then whisk into the flour and salt adding the melted butter last.

2. Spread the mixture thinly onto a baking mat or baking parchment, scatter with both types of sesame seeds and a little Maldon salt.

3. Bake at 175°C until golden and crisp; about 8 minutes, then cool and store in an airtight container until needed.

For the red pepper

1. Heat the grill to maximum and brush the pepper with a little olive oil. Grill the pepper on each side until the skin blisters and scorches a little. When the pepper is cool enough to handle scrape away the blistered skin, remove the stem and seeds and cut the pepper flesh into pieces about 1cm square. Season the pepper squares with salt and a little olive oil and reserve.

For the crab mix

1. Check the crab for any shell or cartilage then combine with 2 teaspoons of lemon juice and enough mayonnaise to bind the crab together.

2. Transfer to a piping bag fitted with a 1½cm nozzle. Keep in the fridge until needed.

To finish and serve

1. Place a rectangle of smoked salmon on each of 4 cold plates. Pipe a line of crab mix along the centre then place 4 pieces of red pepper along the top with a little caviar.

2. Break the taco into shards and press into the crab mixture, finish with the salad shoots and herbs.

The inspiration for this presentation came to me whilst eating at Alinea in Chicago.

Caramelised Veal Sweetbreads, Potato Galette, Broad Beans, Girolles Truffled Madeira Jus

Serves 4

Ingredients

For the sweetbreads

4 x 100g pieces of veal sweetbread, soaked in several changes of cold water for 24 hours

1 clove of garlic

½ onion, roughly chopped

1 small carrot, peeled and chopped

1 stick of celery, roughly chopped

10 white peppercorns

2 bay leaves

2 sprigs thyme

A few parsley stalks

A good pinch of salt

1½ litres of water

For the garnish and sauce

4 tbsp podded baby broad beans, white shells removed

4 tbsp small girolles or other wild mushroom, washed

1 small shallot, peeled and finely chopped

4 galette potatoes (See Essential Basics section)

2 tsp chopped chives

4 slices fresh truffle

1 tsp finely chopped truffle

6 tbsp Madeira sauce (See Essential Basics section)

100g butter

2 tsp olive oil

3 tbsp plain flour with a pinch of salt mixed in

1 clove garlic, cracked

1 sprig of thyme

Method

For the sweetbreads

1. Bring the water to the boil with all of the vegetables, herbs, peppercorns and salt. Simmer for 10 minutes then add the sweetbreads and reduce the heat to a low simmer, cooking until they are firm but still pink inside, for 5-10 minutes. Remove from the heat and allow to cool in the liquid.

2. When cool, remove the sweetbreads from the liquid and peel away any membrane and fat that you find. Dry the sweetbread and store in the fridge until needed.

To finish the dish and serve

1. Prepare the galette potatoes as described in the Essential Basics section, Keep warm until needed.

2. Coat each piece of veal sweetbread in flour lightly and shake off the excess. Heat a non-stick pan over a moderate heat with a little olive oil and lay each sweetbread in the pan. Cook until you have a nice golden crust on the first side, then turn over.

3. Add a decent knob of butter and the garlic and thyme to the pan then continue to cook the sweetbreads, basting them with the aromatic butter.

4. This process will give a golden brown exterior and a moist centre to the sweetbreads.

5. Remove them from the pan to rest while you finish the garnish.

6. Using the same pan discard the butter and aromatics and wipe the pan clear. Add another knob of butter and gently sauté the chopped shallot for 1 minute then add the girolles and a pinch of salt. Cook for a further 1 minute then add the cooked broad beans and chives to the pan and remove from the heat.

7. Warm the sauce with the diced truffle.

8. Place 1 sweetbread at the centre of each plate with a slice of truffle on top then spoon the broad beans and girolles around, place the potato galette alongside. Finally spoon the truffle sauce around and serve.

Cep and Roasted Quail Tart with Green Bean, Artichoke and Hazlenut Salad

Serves 4

Method

1. Roll out the puff pastry to about the thickness of a 50 pence piece and place on a baking tray lined with parchment paper. Place another sheet of parchment on top and another tray on top of that. Bake at 175°C until the pastry is golden and crisp, about 15 minutes. The second tray will stop the pastry rising too much.
2. Cut 4 rectangles of pastry large enough to accommodate a quail leg and breast on each. Put to one side on a baking tray.
3. Cook the quail eggs in boiling water for about 2-3 minutes depending on their size. Then transfer to iced water to stop the cooking process.
4. When cooled, carefully peel the eggs and rinse away any shell fragments.
5. Cut the artichokes into sections and mix the hazelnut oil with the vinegar and chopped nuts.

To cook the quails

1. Brush the quails with melted butter and season with salt and pepper.
2. Roast in the oven at 200°C for 10-12 minutes. Remove from the oven and rest in a warm place for 10 minutes before serving.

To finish and serve

1. Spread a spoonful of warm cep compote on each tart base. Carefully remove the legs and breast from the quails.
2. Place one leg and one breast on each tart base and warm in the oven at 180°C for a minute of two.
3. Meanwhile dress the beans, artichokes, cep slices and rocket with the hazelnut vinaigrette mixture. Divide this between the 4 plates and place the warmed tarts alongside. Cut the top off each egg and place amongst the salad.

Ingredients

For the tarts

2 large quails
2 tbsp melted butter
150g frozen puff pastry, all butter
4 tbsp cep compote (see page 145)
4 quails eggs

For the salad

100g French beans cut into 2.5cm pieces
1 small fresh cep, sliced, optional
4 baby artichokes, cooked (See Essential Basics section)
A few rocket leaves
1 tbsp toasted chopped hazelnuts
2 tbsp hazelnut oil
½ tbsp white wine vinegar

This is a dish full of textures, temperatures and robust earthy flavours.

Ceps on toast with Summer Truffle

Serves 4

Ingredients

150g fresh ceps (small are best),
briefly washed and dried well

1 clove garlic peeled and left whole

1 tbsp olive oil

50g butter

1 small summer truffle, optional

2 tsp chopped parsley

1 tsp cep or porcini oil

2 slices Brioche, cut into 4 rectangles

150ml truffled chicken jus (See
Essential Basic section)

Method

1. Cut the ceps in half if small or into wedges or slices depending on size.
2. Cut the summer truffle into thin slices if using.
3. Heat a frying pan with the olive oil and add the ceps to the pan with the whole garlic clove. Begin toasting the brioche slices in the meantime.
4. As the ceps begin to brown, add the butter and a little salt, shake the pan so that they cook evenly. When soft, finish with black pepper, chives and cep oil.
5. Arrange the ceps along the toast with some truffle slices and serve immediately with some truffled chicken jus.

Note: We have used ceps here but try whichever wild mushrooms are good and plentiful in any given season.

The essence of Autumn - difficult to beat the aroma of fresh ceps and truffle!

Citrus Cured Organic Salmon with Avocado Purée and Sevruga Caviar

Serves 4

Method

For the cured salmon

1. Peel the skin and pith away from the flesh of the oranges and grapefruits then cut 4 segments from each and reserve for the garnish.

2. Slice the rest of the fruit thinly and reserve it.

3. Combine the salt, sugar, spices and dill.

4. Lay a large sheet of cling film over a stainless steel or glass tray. Lay half the fruit slices on top of the cling film to approximate the shape of your salmon. Spread half of the salt mixture over the fruit and follow with the salmon.

5. Top the salmon with the remaining salt followed by the rest of the citrus fruits.

6. Finally, wrap the salmon in the cling film and leave in the fridge for 18-24 hours. When the salmon is firm and the texture even, then it is ready.

7. Rinse the salmon in cold water, discard the marinade, dry the fish and wrap in fresh cling film. Chill for a further 4-6 hours before serving.

For the garnish

1. Peel the avocado and cut into rough pieces. Season with salt, pepper and lemon juice.

2. Place the avocado in the bowl of a liquidiser and add the water on a high speed to give a smooth purée.

3. Cut the reserved citrus segments into triangular sections and reserve.

4. Pick small sprigs from the chervil and dill. Cut the chives into long sections.

To finish

1. Cut the salmon into slices about ½cm thick and lay 2 on each plate. Season the slices with a little sea salt and pepper.

2. Arrange the citrus fruits, avocado, caviar and herbs along the length of the 2 slices and serve.

Ingredients

For the salmon and cure

300g piece of organic salmon, skinned and boned

80g coarse salt

120g granulated sugar

6g juniper berries, chopped

6g white peppercorns, crushed

½ bunch fresh dill, coarsely chopped

1 pink grapefruit

1 orange (This includes some for the garnish)

For the garnish

The reserved citrus segments

25ml water

½ an avocado

1 tsp lemon juice

Salt and white pepper

Small tin of Sevruga or Avruga caviar

A selection of herbs from chervil, dill and chives

Here the citrus counteracts the richness of the salmon, giving a great balance with the salty caviar.

Crispy Duck Egg, White Beans, Chorizo and Black Pudding

Serves 4

Method

For the garnish

1. Drain and rinse the beans, cover with fresh water and simmer with the garlic, shallot and thyme for 1½-2 hours until tender. Add salt at the end of the cooking time and keep warm in the cooking liquid.

2. Dice the confit tomato to the same size as the chorizo.

For the eggs

1. Bring a pan of water to a simmer and add the vinegar. Prepare an ice bath.

2. Crack the eggs into a bowl being careful not to break the yolks. Slip your hand under 1 of the yolks and lift it out of the bowl leaving the white behind. Gently drop the yolk into the simmering water. Repeat quickly with the rest of the eggs. (Use the whites for another dish).

3. Allow the yolk to poach gently for around 2-3 minutes. They should be set around the outside but completely liquid in the centre. When you are happy that this is the case, use a slotted spoon to lift them into the ice bath where you will leave them until completely chilled – about 10 minutes.

4. Drain the egg yolks on kitchen paper and prepare the coating.

5. Arrange 3 bowls – 1 of flour, 1 of beaten hens egg and 1 of crumb and chopped parsley mixed.

6. Pass each yolk through each bowl, first the flour, then egg, then crumbs to give a good coating of crumbs and parsley for each. Reserve the coated yolks in the fridge.

To finish and serve

1. Heat the sunflower oil to 180°C. Remove the eggs from the fridge 20 minutes before cooking them so that they are not too chilly at the centre.

2. Heat 1 tablespoon olive oil in a saucepan, and sauté the chorizo for 1 minute, then stir in 4 tablespoons beans and 1 tablespoon of their cooking liquid. When the beans are thoroughly hot add the diced confit tomatoes, parsley and butter. Stir gently to amalgamate the butter and keep warm.

3. Fry the black pudding slices in a hot non-stick pan with the remaining tablespoon of olive oil. Meanwhile deep fry the eggs until crisp and golden. Drain the eggs and black pudding on kitchen paper.

4. Spoon some of the bean mixture onto warm plates, season the eggs with salt and place next to the beans with the black pudding.

Ingredients

1 litre sunflower oil

4 duck eggs

8 tbsp coarse breadcrumbs (or Japanese Panko crumbs)

1 chicken egg

4 tbsp plain flour and pinch salt

1 tbsp chopped parsley

3 tbsp vinegar

For the garnish

3 tbsp dried haricot beans, soaked overnight in 3 times their volume of cold water

1 shallot

1 clove garlic

1 sprig thyme

1 tbsp chopped chorizo

2 petals of tomato confit (See Essential Basics section)

1 tsp chopped parsley

4 slices black pudding

2 tbsp olive oil

50g butter

Much abused and wholly underrated, the simple green salad has the power to refresh and reinvigorate the appetite during even the most challenging meal.

Green Salad

Serves 4 as a starter

Method

For the green salad

1. Separate the leaves of each of your chosen salads, discarding any damaged or tough outer leaves.
2. Gently wash in cold water. Once may be enough but check and wash again if needed.
3. Dry in a salad spinner. Pull each type of leaf gently into pieces of a manageable size and drop into a roomy bowl. Sprinkle over the sliced shallot and herb leaves followed by your chosen dressing, salt and pepper. The olive oil vinaigrette must be shaken or whisked very well before using.
4. Once assembled, turn the leaves over once or twice very gently to coat and mix. Serve immediately.

For the olive oil vinaigrette

1. Simply whisk everything together in a bowl or shake together in a bottle or a screw top jar.
2. Shake or whisk well before use.

For the creamy lemon vinaigrette

1. Combine the egg yolks with everything except the grapeseed oil and the herbs (optional) in a bowl.
2. Whisk to combine then gradually whisk in the grapeseed oil to form a creamy emulsion.
3. The dressing should be the consistency of double cream – adjust with water if necessary.

Green salad golden rules

- *Choose firm, crisp heads of lettuce for the best texture in the salad.*
- *Handle very gently and as little as possible so as not to bruise the leaves.*
- *Use a salad spinner – soggy lettuce deteriorates fast.*
- *Dress the salad at the last minute before serving.*
- *Only apply enough dressing to make the salad shine – any more will cause premature wilting.*
- *Buy the best quality oils and vinegars. They make all the difference and a little goes a long way.*

Ingredients

For the green salad

1 shallot, peeled and very thinly sliced

4 big (but tender) handfuls of very fresh leaves. Choose any of the following on their own or in combination:

Oakleaf lettuce, Lamb's lettuce, Webb's Wonder, Baby spinach, Small cos, Radiccio (it's not green – but be flexible!), Baby gem, Escarole, Curly endive, Chicory, Lollo Biondo or Rosso as you prefer, Purslane

Also a good sprinkling of herb leaves from the following: Chervil, dill, torn basil, tarragon, flat leaf parsley, chives (cut in 2 inch sticks)

Olive oil vinaigrette

50ml white wine vinegar

250ml extra virgin olive oil

Pinch salt

Smaller pinch sugar

Squeeze of lemon juice

Note: This will keep for several weeks in the fridge

Creamy lemon vinaigrette

3 egg yolks

300ml grapeseed oil

2 tbsp lemon juice

1 tsp sugar

1 tsp grain mustard

1 tsp Dijon mustard

Pinch salt

Pinch white pepper

1 tbsp chopped mixed herbs, optional

Note: This can be kept for up to 1 week in the fridge

Pan fried Calves Liver, Wilted Spinach, Pine Kernels, Lemon and Sage

Serves 4

Ingredients

4 slices of calves liver (about 125g-140g each)

2 tbsp flour with a pinch of salt, combined

2 tbsp sunflower oil

1 tbsp butter, optional

For the garnish and sauce

3 handfuls washed baby spinach

½ tbsp butter

1 lemon

1 tbsp pine kernels, toasted

Small bunch sage

75ml sunflower oil

1 shallot, peeled and sliced

150ml chicken stock (See Essential Basics section)

50ml veal demi-glace (See Essential Basics section)

50g butter

Method

For the garnish

1. Pick a dozen or so nice sage leaves and fry in moderately hot sunflower oil until crisp. Drain well on kitchen towel.

2. Segment the lemon as set out in the recipe for sea bream with citrus fruits (page 131). Then cut each segment across into 3 or 4 pieces and reserve.

To finish and serve

1. Just before serving, heat a non-stick pan. Coat the liver in the flour and salt mixture shaking off any excess.

2. Fry the liver in a little sunflower oil until nicely brown on each side but still pink inside.

3. Add the butter if using and allow to foam and turn brown. This gives the liver a great colour and a buttery, nutty flavour.

4. Remove the liver to a plate or tray and add the shallots to the buttery pan. Saute for 1-2 minutes then add the chicken stock and veal demi-glace. Boil to quickly reduce to a sauce consistency. Add a few of the remaining sage leaves to the pan towards the end then strain the whole through a fine sieve into a clean pan.

5. Sauté the spinach quickly in a little butter with salt and pepper.

6. Place a spoonful of spinach on each plate with the liver next to it. Sprinkle the liver with pine kernels, lemon dice and fried sage. Pour the sauce around.

Some combinations will always stand the test of time. I first ate this dish at Bibendum on Fulham Road cooked by Simon Hopkinson over 20 years ago!

Crispy Pig's head with Tartare Sauce and Herb Salad

Serves 4

Ingredients

For the crispy pig's head

4 slices of pig's head terrine – each about 1cm thick and weighing about 80g (See Essential Basics section)

2 eggs, beaten

2 tbsp of flour with a pinch of salt

6 tbsp coarse breadcrumbs

4 tbsp sunflower oil

For the sauce & garnish

4 tbsp mayonnaise (See Essential Basics section)

½ tbsp chopped capers

½ tbsp chopped cornichons or gherkins

1 tsp each chopped parsley, tarragon, chives, chervil

1 tsp Dijon mustard

1 handful picked and washed salad leaves together with a few leaves from the herbs

1 small shallot, peeled and finely sliced

A little olive oil vinaigrette (See Essential Basics section)

Method

Preparing the pig's head terrine for cooking

1. Arrange a bowl each of flour, beaten egg and breadcrumbs.
2. Pass each slice of terrine in turn through the flour, (tapping off any excess), then the egg and finally the crumbs.
3. Place the coated slices on a tray which has been liberally sprinkled with crumbs to prevent them sticking. Reserve in the fridge.

For the sauce and to finish and serve

1. Combine all the sauce ingredients. Adjust the seasoning to your taste
2. Heat a non-stick pan over a moderate heat and fry the slices of terrine in the sunflower oil until crisp and golden on the first side then turn and repeat on the other
3. Drain the slices on kitchen towel while you dress the salad with the vinaigrette
4. Place a spoonful of the sauce at the centre of each plate with the terrine and salad on top

Ravioli of Foie Gras and Port Sauce

Serves 4

Ingredients

8 x 25g pieces of fresh foie gras

200g pasta dough (See Essential Basics section)

1 egg beaten

300ml Port sauce (See Essential Basics section)

1 tbsp chopped chives

50g butter

Method

For the raviolis

1. Season the nuggets of foie gras with salt and white pepper, cover with cling film and leave at room temperature for 30 minutes.

2. Using a pasta machine, roll the dough out to the finest setting to give a long sheet. Cover the sheet with cling film and leave to rest on the table for 10 minutes. This will prevent the dough from shrinking back later.

3. When its resting time is up, remove the cling film and cut 16 discs of pasta using a 70mm pastry cutter.

4. Brush 8 of the discs with beaten egg and place a piece of foie gras in the centre. Place a plain (not egg washed) disc of pasta on top and press together to seal the edges. Repeat with all the ravioli.

5. Line a tray with cling film to prevent sticking, place the finished raviolis on top and store in the fridge covered with more cling film until required.

To finish and serve

1. Bring a large pan of salted water to the boil and drop in the raviolis. Stir carefully to ensure none sticks to another then leave to simmer for about 3 minutes.

2. Meanwhile, heat the Port sauce.

3. The ravioli is ready when the pasta is tender and the foie gras feels soft through the pasta. Transfer the ravioli to a pan broad enough to accommodate them in a single layer. Dot with the butter and a tablespoon of the cooking water then swirl the pan for about a minute. This will emulsify the butter with the water and coat the raviolis.

4. Season with salt and black pepper to taste, sprinkle the chives over and immediately place 2 on each plate with a little of the chive butter.

5. Finish with the Port sauce and serve.

Note: For added luxury add a little chopped truffle to the sauce.

This dish I first tasted in France. It's simple - two or three ingredients, but an explosion of flavours... absolutely delicious.

Risotto of Goat Cheese, Piquillo Pepper and Rocket with Sweet and Sour Cherry Tomatoes

Serves 4

Method

For the risotto

1. In a medium saucepan, heat 1 tablespoon of olive oil over a moderate heat. Add the onion and garlic to the pan and cook gently without colour until completely soft, or about 6-8 minutes. Add the rice to the pan and cook for 3-4 minutes, stirring constantly. Add the wine and reduce until almost dry. Add enough stock to just cover the rice and simmer, stirring often. Add more stock as you go to keep the rice submerged and continue cooking. The rice should be ready after about 18 minutes but sample to make sure.

2. When ready, remove from the heat and add the peppers, followed by 80g of the goat's cheese and the butter, stirring in gently so as not to damage the rice grains. The consistency should be soft enough to flow slightly but should not be too runny; adjust as necessary with the remaining stock.

3. Finally add the chopped rocket, spoon into warm bowls, scatter with the reserved cheese and the warm marinated tomatoes and a few rocket leaves. Finish with a drizzle of olive oil.

Ingredients

200g Arborio risotto rice

60g onion, finely chopped

½ tsp garlic, chopped

Small glass of dry white wine

900ml of hot vegetable stock (See Essential Basics section)

140g goat's cheese, crumbled

90g butter

1 tbsp chopped fresh rocket and a few whole leaves to garnish

3 tbsp chopped piquillo pepper (use good quality canned)

3 tbsp olive oil

8 sweet and sour cherry tomatoes (See Essential Basics section)

The tomatoes create a great explosion of colour and flavour through this risotto.

Seared Foie Gras with Peach Chutney, Pickled Peach and Amaretti Biscuits

Serves 4

Method

For the peach chutney

1. Place all the ingredients except the peaches into a pan and simmer, stirring often until you have a thickened compote-like mixture.
2. Add the diced peach flesh and continue to simmer until thickened. Stir regularly to prevent the chutney sticking or burning.
3. When you are happy with the consistency, spoon the chutney into sterilised jars to cool and seal.
4. The chutney will be at its best after a week or so and will keep for several weeks.

For the pickled peach

1. Bring the water, sugar and vinegar to the boil briefly and remove from the heat to cool.
2. Cut the peach into wedges and place into the pickling syrup for 30 minutes. Drain the slices and reserve in the fridge.

To cook the foie gras and serve

1. Heat a non-stick pan over a moderate heat. Season the foie gras on both sides with salt.
2. Place the portions in the pan and cook until nicely browned, flip onto the second side and repeat the browning process.
3. When cooked, the foie gras should be caramelised on each side and moist at the centre.
4. Drain the foie gras well and place a piece on each plate with the chutney and 2 slices of pickled peach.
5. Finish with the amaretti biscuit.

Ingredients

4 slices of foie gras (around 90g each)

2 tbsp crushed amaretti biscuits

White bread rolls (See Essential Basics section)

For the peach chutney

450g stoned peach flesh, cut into rough dice

2 tbsp grated cooking apple

2 ripe tomatoes, coarsely chopped

2 tbsp finely chopped onion

Juice and grated zest of 1 lemon

150g caster sugar

½ tsp ground cinnamon

½ tsp nutmeg

½ tsp white pepper

1 tsp grated fresh ginger

150 ml white wine vinegar

70g whole blanched almonds, coarsely chopped

Generous pinch of salt

For the pickled peach

1 ripe fresh peach, cut into wedges

100ml water

100g sugar

100ml white wine vinegar

Sweet and Sour King Prawn

Serves 4 as an amuse bouche or 1 as a starter

Method

For the garnish

1. Cut the carrot and mouli into very fine strips. This is easiest using a mandolin or similar slicing device. Alternatively, simply cut the vegetables into very thin slices then cut across the slices to give very fine shreds. Mix the carrot, mouli and spring onions together and store in cold water until needed.

To finish and serve

1. Heat the sunflower oil to 180°C, warm the sauce epice in a pan which will accommodate the prawns and have the batter ready along with the plain flour in a small bowl. Drain the vegetable strips.

2. Season the prawns with salt then coat lightly with the plain flour and dip into the tempura batter, allowing any excess to drop back into the bowl. Gently lower each prawn into the hot oil and follow with the next.

3. The prawns should be crispy and cooked through after 1½-2 minutes. Drain them well on kitchen towel then drop them into the warm sauce and coat well. Place each prawn in a glass, sprinkle with the sesame seeds and top with some of the vegetable garnish.

4. To serve as a starter simply place 4 prawns on each plate and top with the sesame and vegetables.

Ingredients

4 king prawn tails, shelled, intestine removed and washed

2 tbsp plain flour

3 tbsp tempura batter (See Essential Basics section)

1 litre sunflower oil

3 tbsp sauce epice (See Essential Basics section)

For the garnish

1 tbsp toasted sesame seeds (a mixture of white and black sesame seeds looks good)

100g piece of mouli radish, peeled

1 medium carrot, peeled

2 slender spring onions

A few coriander leaves

The ultimate amuse bouche - perfect to get the taste buds flowing.

Fresh Tagliatelle with Black Mushrooms

Serves 4 as a starter

Method

1. Roll the rested pasta dough as thinly as possible using a pasta machine or rolling pin. Cut the pasta sheets into narrow ribbons to give tagliatelle and sprinkle with semolina to prevent sticking. Reserve in the fridge.

To finish and serve

1. Bring a large pan of salted water to the boil and place another medium pan over a moderate heat.

2. Stir the pasta into the boiling water to prevent them sticking and immediately gently sauté the mushrooms and shallots in the other pan with half the butter. Season the mushrooms with salt.

3. Once the pasta returns to the boil it should only need 1-2 minutes more – be careful not to overcook it.

4. When cooked, drain the pasta and add to the mushroom pan, shaking to combine everything evenly. Season with salt and black pepper. Finally, shake in the parsley and remaining butter.

5. Roll the pasta around a fork – 1 roll for each person, and serve immediately.

Ingredients

300g fresh pasta dough (See Essential Basics section)

2 tbsp semolina

100g butter

A good handful of washed Trompettes des Morts mushrooms (or any seasonal mushrooms)

½ dstsp chopped shallot

½ dstsp chopped parsley

Salt and black pepper

Rolling pasta is good therapy!

Tuna Carpaccio, Champagne-pickled fruits

Serves 4

Ingredients

300g piece trimmed tuna fillet
Sea salt and black pepper

For the pickled fruits and garnish

200ml water
200ml champagne vinegar
200g sugar
4 strawberries
1 ripe peach
1 plum
1 small courgette
A few small basil leaves
4 tsp lemon oil
1 crispy courgette flower (See Red Mullet recipe page 157)

Method

For the tuna

1. Season the tuna with sea salt and black pepper. Heat a heavy non-stick frying pan over a high heat and sear the tuna in olive oil. Do this quickly so that the tuna remains very rare. Reserve the seared tuna in the fridge.

For the pickled fruits and garnish

1. Bring the water, champagne vinegar and sugar to the boil. When the sugar dissolves, cool the mixture.

2. Cut the fruits and courgette into wedges or appropriate shapes and place in the marinade with a few basil leaves for 2 hours. Then drain them well and dress with a little olive oil.

To finish and serve

1. Cut the tuna into slices and season with salt and pepper.

2. Lay the tuna slices on each plate and arrange the fruits alongside with some petals of crispy courgette flower and basil leaves.

A beautiful light summer dish ideal for a dinner party. Very clean and refreshing. The pickling process is very short, so you can use whichever fruits are in season.

Braised Blade of Beef Bourguinon

Method

1. Ask your butcher to tie the blade – this will keep its shape pert and perky.
2. Roll the blade in the flour and seasoning. Shake off any excess.
3. Heat a pan large enough for the blade (an oval cast iron casserole is ideal) and seal it well on all sides in the vegetable oil. Remove to a tray or plate.
4. Add the vegetables, mushroom and garlic to the pan and sauté until lightly coloured. Add the red wine and boil to reduce by two-thirds then add the stock, herbs and the browned blade.
5. Simmer for 10-15 minutes, skimming away any impurities. The meat should be just covered with the stock. Cover with foil and a tight-fitting lid and place in the oven at 90°C for around 4 hours depending on the size of the blade.
6. When cooked, it should be very tender (a spoon handle should pass through without resistance).
7. Carefully remove the meat to a tray or plate and cover to keep warm and moist.
8. Boil the cooking liquor over a high heat to reduce to a sauce consistency then pass through a fine sieve into a clean pan.
9. Whisk in the butter and reserve the sauce.

For the garnish

1. Cut the bacon into lardons, place in a pan and cover with cold water. Bring to the boil and drain immediately. This will remove any excess salt.
2. Heat a non-stick pan large enough for the garnish to fit in one layer. Sauté the lardons gently in a little vegetable oil – they should become crisp and golden and give up some of their fat. Remove from the pan, leaving the bacon fat behind to cook the onions.
3. Sauté the onions until golden and tender. Reserve them with the bacon. Wipe the pan out and heat with the butter until bubbling. Sauté the mushrooms over a high heat. When golden, return the bacon and onions to the pan and season lightly. (Remember the bacon will be salty).
4. Remove the pan from the heat after a minute or so.
5. Cut the bread into croutons and sauté in a little oil until golden. Drain well on kitchen towel.

To serve and finish

1. Place the blade in the centre of a serving plate (or return it to your now washed casserole dish).
2. Spoon the garnish around, pour over the sauce and finish with the croutons and parsley.
3. Serve the pomme purée from the Essential Basics section alongside.

Ingredients

1 whole blade of beef, trimmed of sinew

2 tbsp plain flour, salt and pepper

2 tbsp vegetable oil

2 carrots, peeled and chopped

4 sticks celery, washed and chopped

1 onion, peeled and chopped

4 cloves garlic, cracked

1 large flat mushroom

Few sprigs of thyme

2 bay leaves

1 bottle full bodied red wine

Approximately 3 litres veal or beef stock (depending on the shape of your cooking vessel)

50g butter

For the garnish

100g small button mushrooms, washed and quartered

100g button onions, peeled

A 100g piece (not rashers) of streaky bacon

1 tbsp chopped parsley

A thick slice of good white bread

1 tbsp vegetable oil

1 tbsp butter

Braised Lamb Shanks with Ras al Hanout, Cracked Wheat, Almonds, Piquillo Peppers, Dried Apricots, Capers and Yoghurt

Serves 4

Ingredients

For the shanks

4 tbsp olive oil

4 lamb shanks from the leg (or 8 of the smaller shoulder shanks)

1 head of garlic cut in half

1 onion, diced

1 carrot, peeled and diced

2 glasses dry white wine

2 tomatoes, quartered

1½ litres of chicken stock

Large sprig each of thyme, rosemary and bay leaf

1 slice of lemon

Pinch of saffron

1½ tsp ras al hanout spice mix (available from delicatessens)

8 dried apricots

3 tbsp runny honey

For the toasted cracked wheat

120g cracked wheat (also called bulghar wheat)

approximately 300ml water

1 tbsp finely chopped preserved lemon (optional)

1 tbsp olive oil

For the garnish

4 good quality tinned piquillo peppers, diced

1 tbsp capers, drained

2 tbsp blanched whole almonds, toasted

Fried parsley leaves (See Essential Basics section)

2 tbsp set greek yogurt

Method

For the shanks

1. In a large casserole dish, sauté the onions, carrots and garlic in the olive oil until golden and lovely. Add the tomatoes and cook for 5 minutes more then add the wine and reduce by three quarters. Add the stock to the pan with the herbs, lemon, saffron and 1 teaspoon of ras al hanout. Bring to the boil, add a little salt then the shanks and simmer for 10 minutes. Skim any foam or grease from the surface then cover the pan with foil and a tight fitting lid to give a really good seal.

2. Place the pan into a moderate oven (120°C) for 2-2½ hours or until the meat is tender. Check the level of the liquid after 1½ hours and top up with more stock or water if necessary. The smaller shoulder shanks will be ready after 1½-2 hours.

3. When cooled, remove the shanks from the pan, cover and keep warm while you attend to the sauce.

4. Strain the cooking liquor into a clean pan. If it is a little thin, boil to reduce it to a sauce consistency then taste and add the other ½ teaspoon of ras al hanout and the dried apricots if you wish. Keep everything warm until needed.

Note: You can cook the shanks up to 2 days in advance. Store them in their cooking juice in the fridge then simply reheat them and proceed as above.

For the cracked wheat

1. Heat a pan large enough to take the cracked wheat in a layer of 2cm or so deep. Tip in the wheat and toast over a moderate heat shaking or stirring the pan frequently.

2. The wheat will darken a little and give off a lovely nutty aroma. This is the time to add the water, a pinch of salt and cover with a lid. Reduce the heat and cook gently until all the water is absorbed and the wheat is tender. Keep warm until needed.

To finish and serve

1. Drizzle the shanks with a little honey and salt. Place them in a moderate to hot oven for 8-10 minutes or until hot and glazed.

2. Meanwhile, add the olive oil to the wheat and the lemon dice if using.

3. In a small pan sauté the almonds in the remaining olive oil then add the piquillo peppers and capers. Season with salt.

4. Place a spoonful of cracked wheat at the centre of each plate with a shank on top. Spoon the almond mixture around followed by some of the sauce. Finish with the Greek yoghurt and the fried parsley leaves.

Cote du Boeuf, Yorkshire Puddings, Roast New Season Carrots and Red Wine Sauce

Serves 2

Ingredients

1 cote du boeuf trimmed (ask your butcher for a single rib cutlet)

2 tbsp beef dripping or vegetable oil

Salt and pepper

1 bunch watercress

1 bunch new season carrots, peeled

150ml red wine sauce (See Essential Basics section)

For the Yorkshire puddings

250g plain flour

Good pinch of salt

5 eggs, beaten together

300ml milk

approximately 100ml water

2 tbsp melted beef dripping or vegetable oil

50g butter

Method

1. Take the beef from the fridge 30 minutes before cooking.
2. Heat a heavy frying pan or roasting tray over a moderate heat.
3. Season the beef all over with salt and black pepper then rest it in the pan on its fat. Allow to render and crisp for around 10 minutes.
4. Increase the heat and brown the beef very well on each side. Place into the oven at 180°C and cook for about 8 minutes on each side. Depending on the thickness of your cut, this will give medium-rare beef.
5. When the meat is done to your liking, remove from its pan or tray and leave to rest somewhere warm for a minimum of 20 minutes before carving. This gives time to bake the Yorkshire puddings.

For the garnish and Yorkshire puddings

1. Place the flour and salt in a bowl and gradually whisk in the eggs, water and milk to give a smooth batter. The batter should be the consistency of double cream; adjust with water as necessary. Leave the batter to rest for 30 minutes or overnight.
2. Heat a Yorkshire pudding tray in a 200°C oven until very hot. Carefully spoon a little dripping or vegetable oil into each indent and return to the oven for 5 minutes.
3. Carefully pour enough batter into each indent to fill three-quarters. Return to the oven and bake for 20-25 minutes or until risen, crisp, and standing upright.

For the carrots

1. Place the carrots in a single layer in a pan for which you have a tight-fitting lid. Add enough water to barely cover, together with a pinch of salt and sugar and a knob of butter.
2. Cover the pan and simmer until the carrots are half cooked, then remove the lid. Continue cooking until all the water has evaporated and the carrots have browned nicely in the butter.

To serve

1. If necessary, place the beef in a hot oven for a few minutes to heat through.
2. When sufficiently hot, re-season with salt and pepper and place on a serving platter with the garnish alongside and the sauce in a jug.

Roast Crown of Gressingham Duck, Turnip Fondant, Peach, Duck Croustillant, Red Wine & Lavender Jus

Serves 4

Method

To prepare the ducks and duck croustillants

1. Start one day in advance.
2. Remove the legs from the ducks, season with salt and refrigerate overnight.
3. Leave the breasts on the bone and lightly score any fat with a sharp knife. Refrigerate until needed.
4. The next day heat the duck fat, garlic and thyme, add the duck legs and cook in the oven at 95°C for around 3 hours or until the meat is completely tender and will fall from the bone easily.
5. Remove the legs from the fat. When cool enough to handle, pick the meat from the bones and reserve. Discard the skin and bones.
6. If using foie gras, combine it with the duck leg meat and the quatre epice. Season with salt as necessary. The mixture should have the texture of a coarse pâté.
7. Form the mixture into 4 cigar shapes about 6cm long and 1cm thick.
8. Cut the filo or brik pastry into rectangles 7cm wide by 10cm long.
9. Brush each rectangle with beaten egg over two thirds of its length. Place each portion of the filling at the egg washed end of the rectangle and roll up to wrap in pastry.
10. Leave the non-egg washed third of the pastry as a "tail" and store in the fridge until needed.

For the turnips

1. Peel the turnips and trim to give 4 discs. Use a pastry cutter to neaten the edges if you like.
2. Cook the turnip discs in boiling salted water until just tender. Remove to iced water (this will halt the cooking process).
3. Drain the turnips well.
4. Heat the sugar in a deep pan over a moderate flame until a golden caramel forms. Add the water carefully – it will splutter fiercely – until all of the caramel is dissolved.
5. Add the spice and orange juice and simmer for 2-3 minutes or until a syrupy texture. Stir in the butter.
6. Place the turnip discs into the hot caramel to heat through just before serving, finish with a little salt and pepper after draining them.

To cook the duck breasts

1. Heat the oven to 250°C, remove the duck from the fridge 30 minutes before cooking.
2. Brush the ducks with sunflower oil, season with salt and roast for approximately 12 minutes then remove to a warm place to rest for 30-40 minutes.

To finish and serve

1. Heat the red wine sauce and crumble a few lavender flowers into it. Infuse for 10 minutes then strain through a fine sieve.
2. Cut the peach into wedges and brush with a little butter and sprinkle with sugar. Warm them through gently under the grill.
3. Remove the duck breasts from the bone and re-warm in the oven briefly.
4. Cook the bok choi over a moderate heat in the remaining butter and deep fry the croustillants in sunflower oil at 180°C until crisp. Drain both the bok choi and croustillants well. Season with salt.
5. Cut each duck breast into 2, sprinkle with a few lavender flowers and season with salt and pepper.
6. Arrange the duck on warmed plates with the garnish and spoon the red wine and lavender sauce around.

Ingredients

2 whole Gressingham Ducks
800g duck fat
2 cloves garlic, cracked
1 large sprig of thyme
100ml red wine sauce (See the Essential Basics section)
A few sprigs of fresh lavender

For the croustillants

The cooked duck meat
4 sheets filo pastry (or feuille de brik)
½ tsp quatre epice
50g foie gras diced, optional
1 egg, beaten
1 litre sunflower oil

For the garnish

12 leaves of baby bok choi
1 ripe peach
30g butter melted
Pinch of caster sugar

For the turnips

2 large or 4 small turnips
4 tbsp caster sugar
1 tsp quatre epice
The juice of 1 orange
120ml hot water
30g butter

Fillet of Aberdeenshire Beef cooked on the bone, Snails, Haggis, Garlic and Parsley with Duck Fat Chips

Serves 4

Method

For the fillet steaks

Note: It is difficult to cook a steak at home the way a chef can with professional equipment. Our stoves are far more powerful and our pans heavier. However, it is possible to get close if you have a very heavy frying pan; either cast iron or steel and you don't mind a little smoke.

1. Heat heavy frying pan until very hot and smoking.

2. Season steaks on 1 side with salt and brush with olive oil. Lay the seasoned side onto the pan to begin searing the steak. Do not overcrowd the pan – the steaks will not brown properly unless they have an inch or so of space around them. If the pan is tight then cook the steaks 2 at a time.

3. Cook the steak on the first side for 4-6 minutes or until it has a good brown colour and has begun to cook through. You may need to add a little more oil to the pan from time to time.

4. When you are happy with its progress, season the second side of the steak with salt, turn it over and continue searing for a further 4-6 minutes. These timings will give you a cooking degree around rare or medium rare depending on the thickness of your steaks and other variables (power of stove/temperature of meat before cooking). If you like your steaks cooked more, then extend the cooking time for each side or finish the cooking in a hot oven.

5. When the steaks are cooked to your preference, add the butter, garlic and thyme to the pan and bathe them in the resulting garlicy, thymey, foamy butter for about a minute. Transfer them to a tray or plate, pouring the contents of the pan over the steaks. Reserve somewhere warm but not hot.

For the haggis

1. Peel the skin from the haggis and cut it into 1cm squares.

2. Fry the haggis in a hot pan with a little sunflower oil to brown the cubes well, stirring occasionally. The haggis will begin to break down into a coarse pâté-like texture. Continue frying and turning until the whole mixture has darkened and caramelised a little.

3. At this point, reduce the heat and begin adding the veal demi glace to the pan a spoon at a time, stirring into the haggis until you have a texture similar to firm porridge. Keep the mixture covered and warm until needed.

To finish and serve

1. Warm your prepared red wine sauce, parsley purée and garlic confit. Ensure your haggis and steaks are still hot. Drain your snails and pat dry.

2. Heat the duck fat to 180°C for the chips and fry them until crisp and golden. Meanwhile sauté the snails in butter with the chopped garlic, a little salt and pepper.

3. Place a spoon of haggis on each plate, re-season the steaks and place on top with the chips, garlic confit and snails around. Spoon the red wine sauce around and follow with a ribbon of parsley purée and some deep fried parsley.

Ingredients

4 x 9oz fillet steaks on the bone (or 6oz tornedos)

2 tbsp olive oil

1 tbsp butter

1 sprig thyme

1 clove garlic, cracked

Snails (See Essential Basics section)

For the garnish and sauce

2 tbsp sunflower oil

150g good quality haggis

150g veal demi glace (See Essential Basics section) or brown beef stock

Deep fried parsley (See Essential Basics section)

4 cloves of garlic confit (See Essential Basics section)

4 tbsp parsley purée (See Essential Basics section)

4 portions chips (See Essential Basics section)

4 portions red wine sauce (See Essential Basics section)

Fillet of Halibut, Sweet and Sour Cherry Tomatoes, Portland crab, Orzo, Romaine lettuce and Crab jus

Serves 4

Method

To cook the halibut

1. Brush each portion of fish with lemon oil and place in an oven at 80°C (or into a steamer) and cook for about 8-10 minutes.

For the garnish

1. Cook the orzo in boiling salted water until tender (about 8 minutes) then drain well. Mix with the butter and keep warm in the pan with a lid.

2. Warm the tomatoes in a little of their marinade in the oven.

To finish and serve

1. Remove the fish from the oven or steamer, season with salt and brush with a little more lemon oil.

2. Cook the Romaine lettuce in a hot pan with a little olive oil and water. Drain well when wilted and season with salt.

3. Stir the crab meat into the hot pasta, ensure the crab sauce is hot and add 2-3 tablespoons of the sauce to the orzo to give a risotto consistency.

4. Plate the lettuce at the centre of each plate with the halibut on top, a spoon of orzo alongside with the warm tomatoes on top.

5. Serve the rest of the sauce separately.

Ingredients

2 tbsp lemon oil (or olive oil)

4 x 150g portions of halibut, skin and bones removed

For the garnish

12 marinated cherry tomatoes (See Essential Basics section)

100g orzo pasta (or rosmarino)

100g white crab meat

50g butter

1 Romaine lettuce

1 tbsp olive oil

200ml crab jus (See Essential Basics section)

Fillet of Pork, Butternut Squash Purée, Black Pudding, Crispy Pig's Head and Capers

Serves 4

Method

For the garnish

1. Peel the butternut squash and cut into slices about as thick as a 50 pence piece. From these slices cut small discs using an apple corer or small pastry cutter. You will need 2 tablespoons of discs. Alternatively, cut the butternut squash into neat cubes or a shape of your choice.
2. Cook the butternut discs or cubes in boiling, salted water until tender then refresh them in iced water and drain well. Reserve.
3. Take 200g of the butternut and chop roughly for the purée. Cook the butternut in the butter with a pinch of salt, a splash of water and a tight fitting lid over a gentle heat.
4. Check the pan occasionally and add a little more water if it seems dry. Do not allow the butternut to brown at any point as this will spoil the colour of the finished purée.
5. When the butternut is completely tender, add the cream, bring to the boil and remove from the heat.
6. Purée the mixture in a liquidiser then pass it through a fine sieve. Keep the purée warm until needed.

For the crispy pig's head

1. You will need 3 bowls to coat the terrine; 1 with the flour, 1 with the beaten egg and 1 with the breadcrumbs.
2. Pass the cubes of terrine through the flour being careful to coat well but to tap off any excess. Then coat with the egg, again allowing excess egg to drip back into the bowl before coating the cubes in breadcrumbs. Reserve the cubes in the fridge until needed.

To cook the pork fillet

1. Heat a heavy based frying pan over a moderate heat, season the pork fillet with salt and seal in the hot pan with the olive oil.
2. Turn the pork regularly to brown it well on all sides. This should take about 6 minutes.
3. Place the pork in the oven, still in its hot pan and give it about 5 minutes at 180°C turning once about halfway through. A large fillet may need a further 5 minutes and another turn to cook through. The pork fillet will become extremely dry if overcooked so keep it slightly pink.
4. Remove the pan from the oven and add the butter, thyme and the cracked garlic clove. Allow this to bubble and foam and the flavours to become acquainted as you roll the pork back and forth in the pan.
5. When you feel the meat is ready, remove it from the pan to a tray or plate and pour the garlicky, thymey butter over the top. Allow the pork to rest for 10 minutes before carving.

To finish and serve

1. Ensure that the purée, sauce and pork fillet are all hot and that the sunflower oil is heated to 170°C.
2. Fry the black pudding slices in a little olive oil to crisp each side. Meanwhile, fry the cubes of terrine in the sunflower oil until golden and crisp. Drain them and the black pudding on kitchen towel. Heat the butternut discs in a little butter and water in a saucepan. When they are hot, add the capers and chives and remove from the heat.
3. Place a spoon of butternut purée on the left of each hot plate and using a palette knife, spread it to the right of each plate to give a broad ribbon of purée. Arrange all the components along the purée and serve the Madeira sauce in a sauceboat alongside.

Ingredients

800g of pork fillet (trimmed of fat and sinew)

2 tbsp olive oil

12 cubes of pig's head terrine (See Essential Basics section)

1 litre sunflower oil for deep frying

8 slices black pudding

1 clove garlic and 1 sprig of thyme

50g butter

For the garnish and sauce

1 small butternut squash

75g butter

50g cream

150ml Madeira sauce (See Essential Basics section)

1 tbsp capers

2 tsp chopped chives

1 egg beaten

2 tbsp plain flour

4 tbsp coarse bread crumbs

A handful of deep fried parsley leaves (See Essential Basics section)

Fillet of Sea Bass, Wild Rice, Squid, Chorizo Sausage and Red Peppers

Serves 4

Method

For the garnish

1. Soak the rice in warm water for 1 hour before cooking.

2. Drain the rice well, bring 650ml water and a pinch of salt to the boil then add the rice. Reduce to a simmer, cover with a lid and cook gently for about 45 minutes. The rice should absorb all of the water and be tender. Don't worry if the rice grains burst – this is normal. Keep the rice warm.

3. Cut the squid and red pepper into a neat dice but keep them separate.

For the chorizo sauce

1. Place all the ingredients except the lecithin into a saucepan and simmer for 10 minutes. Liquidise the mixture for a few seconds only then pass through a sieve. Discard the solids but keep the chorizo flavoured stock.

2. Using a hand blender, dissolve the lecithin into the hot stock. This will give you a light "moussey" sauce. Keep warm.

To finish and serve

1. Coat the sea bass portions in flour and tap off any excess.

2. Heat the olive oil in a non-stick pan over a moderate heat. Place the fish skin side down into the pan 1 piece at a time. Press each 1 flat with the back of your fish slice before adding the next. This will prevent the skin from contracting and curling the fish.

3. Cook the bass for about 5-7 minutes to give a nice crisp skin then turn over and continue cooking until done. Finish with salt and a squeeze of lemon.

4. Remove the bass from the pan and keep warm. Using the same pan, sauté the red pepper and garlic in a little olive oil until soft but not browned. Add the squid to the pan and season with salt. Cook for 1 minute before adding the chorizo followed by the warm rice after another minute. Finally add the parsley.

To serve

1. Spoon a little rice mixture on top of each piece of bass and spread to cover the surface.

2. Place on a plate and spoon a little sauce around.

Ingredients

4 x 150g pieces of thick sea bass fillet
2 tbsp olive oil
2 tbsp plain flour
Salt
½ a lemon

For the garnish

1 small squid cleaned by your fishmonger (or you could use good quality frozen squid)
2 tbsp olive oil
200g wild rice
650ml water
Pinch of salt
1 red pepper, peeled using a potato peeler
½ clove garlic, chopped
1 tbsp chorizo sausage, diced
2 tsp chopped flat leaf parsley

For the chorizo sauce

75g chorizo trimmings
500ml chicken stock
1 clove garlic, cracked
1 shallot, peeled and sliced
1 dtbsp soya bean lecithin granules (available from Health Food shops)

Fillet of Sea Bream, Endive Marmalade, Grilled Endive, Citrus Sauce with Basil

Serves 4

Method

For the endive

1. Remove 20 nice leaves from the endive, trim to the same length (approximately 8cm) reserve them on a metal tray ready for grilling later.

2. Finely slice the shallots, cut the remaining endive into quarters and trim the root from each quarter. Finely shred the endive with a sharp knife.

3. Cook the shallots gently in the butter with a pinch of salt until translucent and completely soft. Add the endive to the pan with a pinch of salt and sugar, continue to cook gently with a lid until wilted then add the sugar, herb sprigs, lemon juice and white pepper. Replace the lid and continue cooking until completely soft.

4. Remove the lid and pour in the sherry vinegar. Continue cooking without the lid until the vinegar has completely reduced and the mixture is moist but not leeching liquid. Taste and adjust the sugar and/or vinegar as necessary to give a slightly sweet but tangy taste. Keep the marmalade warm until needed.

For the citrus fruits

1. Cut the top and bottom off the orange and grapefruit to expose the flesh at each end. With 1 of the cut ends flat on the chopping board use a sharp knife to remove the skin and pith in strips working top to bottom. Be careful not to cut away too much of the flesh.

2. When both fruits are completely peeled cut either side of the membranes which separate the segments. Allow the segments to drop into a bowl which will also catch any juice from the fruit. Cut the segments across to give large pieces, reserve.

To finish and serve

1. Heat a large non-stick frying pan over a high heat. Coat the bream fillets in the flour and a pinch of salt. Tap off the excess flour.

2. Add a little olive oil to the pan followed by the fish fillets, skin side down. Allow the fish to crisp over a high heat for 4 or 5 minutes then reduce the heat and turn the fish over. It should be nicely browned with a crisp skin.

3. Allow the fish to cook for a further 3 or 4 minutes on the second side then remove from the pan and keep warm on a metal tray.

4. Brush the endive spears with a little olive oil and season with salt and a pinch of sugar. Place under a hot grill to cook for 3-4 minutes.

5. Meanwhile warm the sauce with the citrus fruits and check the endive marmalade is also warm and ready.

6. Place a spoonful of the marmalade on each plate. For a professional finish, place it inside a round pastry cutter and flatten with a spoon. Arrange 5 grilled endives alongside and the crispy fish on top. Spoon around the sauce and citrus fruits and finish with the fresh basil leaves.

Ingredients

4 fillets of gilt head sea bream, trimmed and boned

2 tbsp plain flour

Pinch of salt

4 tbsp olive oil

6 tbsp citrus and basil butter sauce (See Essential Basics section)

For the endive

5 heads of endive

Shallots, peeled

Lemon juice

Butter

Parsley sprig

Tarragon sprig

Sherry vinegar

Sugar

Salt and white pepper

For the garnish

1 large orange

1 pink grapefruit

A few small basil leaves

Fillet of Turbot, White Asparagus, Girolles, Leaf Spinach and New Potatoes, Truffle Chicken jus

Serves 4

Method

For the garnish

1. Wash the potatoes then simmer them in salted water until just tender. Keep them warm in the water.

2. Peel the asparagus and place in a pan in a shallow layer. Add enough water to half cover, together with a dessert spoon of butter a pinch of salt and sugar. Cover with a lid and bring to the boil. Cook until just tender and remove the lid but keep warm.

To cook the turbot and finish the dish

1. Season the turbot with salt then coat in the plain flour, tapping off any excess.

2. Heat a non-stick frying pan over a high heat. Add the vegetable oil followed by the turbot portions and cook until the first side is golden. Turn onto the second side and reduce the heat to moderate.

3. In the meantime, drain the potatoes and sauté with the cracked garlic clove, 1 sprig of thyme and a knob of butter. Re-warm the asparagus in its cooking juice wilt the spinach in a little oil or butter. Also ensure the sauce is hot enough.

4. Add the remaining butter to the turbot pan. Baste the turbot with the foamy butter and remove from the pan when cooked. Keep the turbot warm while you sauté the girolles in the remaining turbot butter. Drain the mushrooms when cooked and season.

5. Arrange the spinach, potatoes, asparagus and mushrooms on each plate with the turbot at the centre and some sauce around.

Ingredients

4 x 125g pieces of turbot fillet

A little vegetable oil for frying

2 tbsp plain flour to coat the fish

50g butter

For the garnish and sauce

12 small new potatoes in their skins

4 spears of white asparagus or 8 if very small

4 handfuls of baby spinach, washed

200g girolles or any good wild mushroom

1 recipe of truffled chicken jus (See Essential Basics section)

4 slices of fresh truffle, optional

4 leaves of baby spinach, reserved for garnish

100g butter

2 sprigs of thyme

1 clove garlic, cracked

A great classic with great basic flavours. You should get a burst of the sea when eating this.

Lobster à la Russe

Method

To cook the lobsters

1. Bring a large pan of salted water to the boil.

2. Using a large cook's knife and with the lobster held firmly on the chopping board, cut briskly through the head along the natural seam in the shell. This will kill the lobster quickly.

3. Break the claws off and remove the head from the tail. Remember to extract and remove the green coral sac from the head if you want to make coral mayonnaise.

4. Plunge the claws into the boiling water and cook for around 3-4 minutes then remove from the water and leave to cool. Cook the tails in the same way for 3 minutes. If your lobsters are particularly large you will need to allow another 1 or 2 minutes cooking for both the claws and tails.

5. When cool, remove the tail meat by cracking the shell with your hands. Cut each tail in half lengthways and remove the intestinal tract from each half.

6. Use a meat bat or small hammer to crack the claws. Carefully extract the claws intact, and rinse the claws and tails under cold water. Dry on absorbent paper and reserve in the fridge.

For the garnish

1. Cook each of the raw vegetables in turn in boiling salted water. Plunge each into cold water just long enough to stop the cooking process. Drain well.

2. In a bowl mix the diced cooked artichoke with the other vegetables and season with salt and pepper. Then add enough mayonnaise to bind the vegetables together. Reserve in the fridge.

For the coral mayonnaise

1. Bring a small pan of water to the boil with a good pinch of salt.

2. Cook the coral in the water for about 3 minutes. It will change from a deep green colour to vivid 'lobster pink' when cooked.

3. Plunge the coral into cold water to stop the cooking process then drain well.

4. Work the mayonnaise, coral and lemon juice in a small liquidiser until smooth then pass through a fine sieve and reserve.

To finish the dish

1. Season the lobster pieces with salt, white pepper, olive oil and lemon juice to create a shine.

2. Place 2 spoonfuls of Russian salad on each plate with the lobster arranged on top.

3. Arrange the herbs salad over and around the lobster.

4. If using coral mayonnaise pipe small dots onto the plate using a piping bag or squeezy bottle.

Ingredients

2 live lobsters (500g – 600g size)

For the garnish

3 tbsp diced potato

3 tbsp diced turnip

3 tbsp diced cooked globe artichoke (See Essential Basics section)

3 tbsp peas

3 tbsp diced French beans

4 tbsp mayonnaise (See Essential Basics section)

A handful of herb salad to include any or all of: chervil, chives, dill, curly endive, baby spinach, olive oil and lemon juice.

For the coral mayonnaise

The coral sack from the back of the lobster head

2 tbsp mayonnaise (See Essential Basics section)

Squeeze of lemon juice

Poulet Basquaise

Serves 4

Ingredients

1 Cotswold white chicken, jointed

1 bunch Grelot onions or bulbous spring onions, cut in half and washed

1 red pepper, deseeded and diced

1 yellow pepper, deseeded and diced

1 small onion, peeled and diced

8 cloves garlic, separated but not peeled

8 Charlotte new potatoes, peeled and thickly sliced

2 thick slices of Bayonne ham or bacon, cut into pieces

2 glasses of dry white wine

3 tomatoes, chopped

A sprig of thyme and bay leaf

A good pinch of Espelette pepper or chilli powder

A pinch of saffron filaments

1 litre chicken stock (See Essential Basics section)

2 tbsp olive oil

1 tbsp butter

2 tsp lemon juice

1 tbsp basil leaves, torn

Method

1. Heat a casserole dish big enough to take the chicken pieces snugly.

2. Season the chicken with salt and brown in the casserole with olive oil. When nicely coloured on all sides remove from the pan and put to one side. You may need to brown the chicken in 2 batches.

3. Add the peppers, both types of onions, the garlic and ham to the casserole and sauté for 5 minutes then add the tomatoes, herbs and spices and white wine. Cook for 5 minutes more.

4. Return the chicken to the casserole and pour in enough chicken stock to barely cover. Bring to a simmer and skim off any impurities. Add the potatoes, cover with a tight-fitting lid and place in a 160°C oven for around 30 minutes or until cooked through.

5. Remove all the chicken and vegetables from the casserole with a slotted spoon and keep warm.

6. Boil the cooking liquor in the casserole to reduce to a sauce consistency then whisk in the butter, lemon juice and basil.

7. Return the chicken and vegetables to the casserole and heat gently together.

8. Serve immediately.

A new generation of quality English chicken - with a classic Basque combination.

Roast Belly of Middlewhite Pork, Fennel Compote, Charlotte Potatoes and Pork Jus

Serves 6

Method

For the pork

1. The day before roasting, score the pork skin with a sharp knife (a Stanley knife is ideal).
2. Mix the crushed spices with the salt and spread half on a tray large enough for the meat. Lay the pork skin side down onto the salt mixture and cover with the remainder.
3. Leave the pork in the fridge for about 4 hours, then brush off and discard the salt mixture. Return the pork to the fridge and leave uncovered skin side up for a minimum of 8 hours or up to 2 days. This will give a salted dry skin which is perfect for crackling.

To cook the pork

1. In a roasting tray big enough for the pork with a little spare space, scatter the onion, fennel trimmings, garlic and thyme. Place the pork on top with the skin uppermost.
2. Rub the vegetable oil into the skin and place the whole thing in a 200°C oven for about 20 minutes, then reduce the heat to 175°C.
3. Continue cooking for about 1½ hours – the skin should be crisp and the flesh soft and tender. When ready, keep warm.

For the garnish and jus

1. Cook the Charlotte potatoes in boiling salted water until tender. Drain and reserve.
2. Spoon a little of the pork fat from the tray into a frying pan (alternatively use duck fat or olive oil). Add the tender potatoes and clove of garlic to the hot fat and sauté together until lightly coloured.
3. Remove the pork from the roasting tray. Place the tray containing all the meat juices and vegetables over a high heat. Reduce and caramelise the contents.
4. Tip off any excess fat then pour in the chicken stock and boil rapidly for about 10 minutes.
5. Pass the liquid through a sieve into another saucepan. Discard the solids and reduce the jus to give a sauce consistency. Keep warm.
6. Heat the fennel compote and check for seasoning.

Note: Cut the pork belly into thick slices and arrange on the plate with the fennel compote, potatoes and a few shavings of raw fennel. Finally, scatter with the chives.

Ingredients

2kg piece of Middlewhite pork belly (skin and bones intact)

2 good handfuls of coarse salt

2 tsp cracked black peppercorns

2 tsp fennel seeds, crushed

3 tbsp vegetable oil

1 onion, peeled and cut into thick slices

2 cloves garlic, cracked

The fennel trimmings from the compote

3 or 4 sprigs thyme

For the garnish and jus

4 good tbsp of fennel compote (See Essential Basics section)

A few shavings of raw fennel reserved in cold water

Charlotte potatoes; 3 or 5 each depending on appetite

1 clove garlic, cracked

A small bunch of chives, cut into 1inch sticks

1½ litres chicken stock

Roast Cotswold White Chicken, Chips and Baby Gem

Serves 4

Ingredients

1 whole Cotswold white chicken

4-6 large Maris piper potatoes (depending on your appetite)

1 litre of duck fat, beef dripping or vegetable oil

2 heads of baby gem lettuce

2 tbsp vinaigrette (See Essential Basics section)

1 head of garlic separated into individual cloves

A few sprigs of thyme

For the jus

2 tbsp each of onion, carrot and celery, all chopped to roughly ½cm size pieces

1 glass dry white wine

1 litre chicken stock (See Essential Basics section)

75g veal demi-glace, optional (See Essential Basics section)

The washed and chopped giblets if you have them

Method

For the chicken

1. Heat your oven to 180°C. Place a sprig of thyme and 2 cracked garlic cloves inside the cavity. To truss your chicken, use a piece of string around 2 feet in length.

2. Tie your chicken's ankles together where they meet at the tip of the breast. This should be done with the halfway point of your piece of string so as to leave about a foot of spare string at each side.

3. Pass the pieces of string across each thigh, down under the body and tie securely pushing the thighs into the body.

Note: Trussing is not entirely necessary but will give a tidy appearance when presented and stops the bird from rolling over when roasting on each side.

4. Season your chicken all over with salt. Heat a heavy roasting tray or a frying pan with a metal handle which will fit into your oven.

5. Add a dessert spoon of duck fat or vegetable oil to the pan then roll your chicken around in the pan to coat with your chosen fat.

6. When nicely coated, position your chicken on 1 or other of its sides and place in the oven.

Note: The bird should rest on its thigh as this allows the heat to penetrate the leg which would normally take longer to cook than the delicate breast meat.

7. After 15 or 20 minutes, turn the chicken onto the other side, again resting on its thigh. Continue roasting for a further 15-20 minutes then add the remaining garlic cloves and thyme to the tray and turn the chicken onto its back i.e. breast uppermost.

8. Return to the oven to finish cooking and allow the breast skin to brown and crisp. This will take around 20 minutes depending on the size of your chicken. When done, the juice should run clear from the leg when pierced with a cocktail stick and the breast should be firm to touch.

9. Remove from the oven and rest the bird for 20 minutes before serving. Reserve the roasted garlic cloves to serve alongside the chicken but keep the tray and contents to make the jus.

For the chicken jus

1. If you have the giblets, add them to the chicken's roasting tray and cook over a high heat for 5-8 minutes. Tip off any excess fat then add the vegetables to the pan and cook for a further 5 minutes. Pour in the wine and boil to reduce by half then add the chicken stock and veal jus if using.

2. Simmer the jus for 10-15 minutes or until reduced and becoming a little syrupy, then pass the liquid through a sieve into a saucepan and discard the solids.

3. If the jus is a little thin, boil to reduce to thicker consistency and keep warm until needed.

For the baby gem lettuce

1. Remove any damaged outer leaves and cut the lettuce into wedges lengthways through the root. Wash briefly in cold water and drain well.

2. Toss the wedges in a bowl with the vinaigrette, salt and pepper.

To finish and serve

1. Heat the oil or fat to 180°C. Heat the chicken jus. Add the chips to the fat. Meanwhile, either carve the chicken or ready it for carving at the table.

2. Arrange the chicken on warmed plates with the dressed baby gem and some roasted garlic. Drain the chips when golden and crisp and place next to the chicken portions. Serve the chicken jus in a sauce boat at the table.

Roast Loin and Slow-cooked Shoulder of Cornish Lamb, Radish, Feta Cheese, Green Beans, Chickpeas and Lovage

Serves 4

Method

To cook the lamb

1. Heat a heavy frying pan or roasting tray over a high heat. Season the lamb with salt and place in the pan fat side down with the vegetable oil.

2. When the fat has become nicely browned, turn the lamb over, add the garlic and thyme and put the pan into the oven at 180°C.

3. Roast for about 8 minutes depending on the size of the loins then remove the lamb to a cool tray. Pour over the garlic and thyme oil from the pan and leave it to rest on a warm plate for 15-20 minutes.

For the garnish

1. Slice 3 of the radishes very thinly and reserve in iced water. Place the remaining radishes in a pan large enough to spread them in a single layer, add a knob of butter, a pinch each of salt and sugar and cover them snugly with a sheet of kitchen parchment trimmed to fit the diameter of the pan.

2. Cook the radishes until just tender then remove from the heat but leave in the pan.

3. Cook the French beans in boiling salted water until tender then refresh in iced water and drain well when thoroughly cold.

To finish and serve

1. Place the lamb shoulder slices into a dry, hot non-stick frying pan. When nicely browned turn onto the other side. The slices should be crisp on the outside and tender in the middle.

2. Meanwhile return the loins to the oven for about 5 minutes to warm through.

3. Heat the beans in the remaining butter, adding the diced feta when they are thoroughly hot.

4. Add the chickpeas to the radish pan and boil to reduce the cooking liquid. This will glaze the radishes and chickpeas nicely. Heat the lamb jus and sprinkle on the chopped lovage.

5. When everything is hot and ready, cut the lamb loin into chunky slices and place next to a slice of crispy shoulder on warmed plates.

6. Spoon the beans, chickpeas and radishes around, top with a few raw radish slices for freshness and finish with the lovage lamb jus.

Ingredients

2 loins of lamb, trimmed but with the fat layer intact

2 cloves garlic, cracked

4 sprigs thyme

2 tbsp vegetable oil

For the garnish

2 tbsp plain flour

4 slices of slow-cooked lamb shoulder (See Essential Basics section)

15 radishes, washed

4 tbsp cooked chickpeas (See Essential Basics section)

50g butter

Pinch of salt and sugar

200g French beans, trimmed

75g feta cheese, diced

150ml basic lamb jus (See Essential Basics section)

1 tbsp chopped lovage leaves

Roast Loin of Venison, Cep Purée, Grelot Onions and Port Sauce

Serves 4

Method

For the cep purée

1. Wash and slice the ceps, heat a medium pan with the butter until bubbling then add the garlic and shallot. Cook over a moderate heat until soft then add the ceps or your mushroom of choice with a pinch of salt. Continue cooking with an occasional stir until the mushrooms have wilted. Add the Madeira and reduce until almost dry then add enough water to just cover the mushrooms.

2. Simmer until the mushrooms are soft then add the double cream and boil to reduce by half.

3. Liquidise the mixture very well and pass through a fine sieve. Adjust the seasoning if necessary and keep warm until needed.

For the grelot onions

1. Trim away any damaged layers from the onions, trim the roots and wash well. Split the onions lengthways into 2 if large – leave whole if small.

2. Heat a non-stick pan large enough to take the onions in a single layer over a moderate to low heat. Add a little olive oil to the pan then place the onions cut side down in the pan to cook. Season with salt then add a few tablespoons of water and cover with a lid. The onions will cook in the steam created; if they are still firm when the water has all gone then add a little more and continue cooking. When tender, remove the lid. The remaining water will evaporate then the onions will begin to fry. They are ready when golden and caramelised. Keep warm until needed.

For the venison

1. Season the venison with salt, sear in a hot frying pan with the oil on all sides until nicely coloured – about 8-10 minutes.

2. Reduce the heat and add the butter, garlic and thyme to the pan. As the butter foams, baste the venison and turn it every couple of minutes. Cook the venison for around 10-12 minutes depending on its thickness.

3. When it is cooked to your liking, remove it from the pan and rest somewhere warm.

To finish and serve

1. Ensure that the purée, sauce, onions and venison are all hot.

2. Heat a small frying pan and sauté the ceps over a high heat with a little olive oil and butter. Season with salt and pepper.

3. Brush a little cep purée on each plate to give a ribbon shape, place the onions and ceps along it with a slice of venison. Spoon the sauce around and the cep oil if you have it.

Ingredients

700g piece of venison loin trimmed of all fat and sinew – at room temperature

2 tbsp sunflower oil

2 tbsp butter

1 garlic clove

1 sprig thyme

For the cep purée

100g fresh ceps or other mushroom of your choice

½ tsp chopped garlic

1 small shallot – peeled and sliced

60ml Madeira

75ml double cream

30g butter

For the garnish and sauce

4 grelot onions or 8 small bulbous spring onions

4 ceps – washed and cut in quarters or other mushroom of your choice

2 tbsp olive oil

1 tbsp butter

Fried parsley leaves (See Essential Basics section)

8 tbsp Port sauce (See Essential Basics section)

1 tbsp cep or porcini oil, optional

The venison we use roam free on the 600 acre Finnebrogue Estate in Northern Ireland – the meat is extremely delicate and tender.

Roast Squab Pigeon, Peas, Button Onions & Bacon

Serves 4

Ingredients

4 squab pigeons (or wood pigeons)
200g shelled fresh peas (or frozen)
8 button onions, peeled
2 thick slices of streaky bacon
2 cloves of garlic, peeled
A few sprigs of fresh thyme
2 tbsp sunflower oil
100g unsalted butter

For the sauce

75ml white wine
75ml Madeira
200ml veal demi glace (See Essential Basics section)
1 shallot, peeled & sliced
A small knob of butter
A large sprig of thyme

Method

For the squab pigeon and the sauce

1. Remove any feathers or stubble which may have been overlooked.
2. Season the birds inside and out, then brown all over in a hot frying pan with a little vegetable oil.
3. When you have a good colour, place the pigeons on their backs and add the garlic and thyme to the pan along with 50g of the butter.
4. Baste the pigeons with the butter and roast for 10-12 minutes in a hot oven (200°C).
5. Remove the pigeons onto a plate to rest and pour any excess grease from the pan.
6. Add the sliced shallot and a little butter to the garlic and thyme in the pan, and sauté for 3-4 minutes.
7. When the shallots are slightly browned and softened, add the wine and Madeira. Reduce by half, then add the veal demi-glace and thyme.
8. Simmer the sauce until you have a light coating consistency, then pass through a sieve.
9. Whisk in a little butter and keep the sauce warm.

For the garnish

1. Cut the bacon across into strips and place in a small pan of water. Bring to the boil and drain immediately.
2. Sauté the bacon lardons with a little vegetable oil in a small frying pan until golden and giving up some of their fat.
3. Remove the bacon from the pan leaving some of the fat behind.
4. Cut the button onions in half and cook very gently, cut side down, until nicely browned. Turn and continue cooking until soft to the point of a knife.
5. Season the onions with a little salt, then return the bacon to the pan and keep warm.
6. Just before serving, cook the peas in boiling salted water for a minute or 2. Drain well and season with salt, a little sugar, and white pepper. Stir in a knob of butter.

To finish and serve

1. Ensure the sauce, peas and garnish are all warmed.
2. Return the pigeons to the oven for 2-3 minutes to heat through.
3. To serve, simply place a whole pigeon on each plate with the peas, onions and bacon or alternatively remove the legs and breasts from each bird and arrange them with the garnish.
4. Serve the sauce separately.

My favourite meat, subtle, juicy and velvety. It must be eaten pink, but as long as it's cooked correctly it's very versatile.

Seared Scallops, Red Peppers, Espelette, Sweetcorn, Squid and Lime with Coriander

Serves 4

Method

For the scallops

1. Ask your fishmonger to remove the scallops from the shell and trim away the beard, roe and any membrane.
2. Wash the scallops briefly but thoroughly in cold water. Dry them well and store in the fridge until ready to cook.

For the garnish

1. Heat the oven to 250°C. Brush the peppers lightly with a little olive oil then place them on a rack over a tray in the oven for about 8-10 minutes or until the skins blister a little and can be peeled off.
2. Plunge the peppers into ice water for 5 minutes then drain.
3. Peel the peppers, remove the seeds and stalk and cut into rectangular pieces or dice as you wish. Reserve the peppers.
4. Remove the sweetcorn kernels from the cob using a sharp knife then cook in boiling salted water for 2 minutes. Drain and plunge into ice water to stop them overcooking. Drain well and reserve.
5. Pick and wash the coriander (4-5 leaves). Cut the lime in half and reserve.

To finish

1. Heat a non-stick frying pan. Add a spoonful of olive oil and sear the scallops for approximately 2 minutes. When nicely coloured, turn them over and cook the other side. Add the squid to the pan, season with salt and continue cooking for about another minute. The squid should be lightly coloured but will toughen if overcooked and likewise the scallops should be medium rare.
2. While the scallops are cooking, heat the corn and red pepper pieces in a separate pan with a little olive oil, salt and espelette.
3. Place the cooked scallops onto warmed plates. Add the squid to the peppers and corn then squeeze over a little lime juice. Spoon the squid and garnish around the scallops and finish with a few coriander leaves, olive oil and a little shredded lime zest.

Ingredients

8 large scallops, preferably hand-dived

2 baby squid, cleaned and cut into rings

1 large or 2 small red peppers

1 cob of fresh sweetcorn

Fresh coriander to garnish

1 lime

Extra virgin olive oil

A pinch of ground Espelette or cayenne pepper

The sweetness of scallops, roasted pepper and sweetcorn balanced with Espelette pepper and lime.

Slow cooked Aberdeenshire Beef, Glazed carrots and Potato Purée

Serves 4

Method

Salting the ox cheeks

1. Mix the salt and black pepper together. Place half in a tray or bowl that will take the ox cheeks snugly. Top with the cheeks then cover with the remaining salt, working it between them too. Cover with cling film and leave in the fridge overnight. The next day, discard the salt and rinse the cheeks briefly in cold water. Pat them dry and reserve until needed. They will be fine for upto 2 days in the fridge once salted so you can get them ready in advance of cooking.

Cooking the cheeks

1. Heat a heavy casserole over high heat with a little sunflower oil and sear the ox cheeks on all sides to give a nice roasted surface to each piece. Remove them from the pan.

2. Using the same pan and a little more oil, fry the garlic cloves until turning golden then add the carrot, onion and celery. Frying for a further 8 minutes or so before adding the leeks tomatoes and mushrooms.

3. Continue cooking until the vegetables have softened a little and the tomatoes have broken down. Then add the Madeira and red wine and boil to reduce by three quarters. Return the ox cheeks to the pan and cover with the stock. Bring to the boil and simmer for 10 minutes. Skim excess oil from the surface then add the herbs and juniper berries cover tightly with a sheet of foil and a heavy lid to give a really tight seal.

4. Cook the ox cheeks in a low oven (about 120°C) for about 4 hours or until completely melting and tender. You should be able to eat the ox cheeks with a spoon if properly cooked.

5. Remove from the oven when cooked and either cool in the liquid and refrigerate to use another day or if you want to eat directly, remove the ox cheeks from the pan cover and reserve. Strain the cooking juice into another pan and check the consistency. It should be a shiny coating texture but not too thick. Adjust the sauce either by reducing or thinning with water.

6. When you are happy with the sauce return the meat to it, cover and keep hot until needed.

For the garnish

1. Slice the carrots thinly and place in a pan in a shallow layer. Add enough water to barely cover, add the butter, a pinch of salt and sugar.

2. Place over a high heat covered with a lid and boil for 3-4 minutes before removing the lid. Continue boiling, shaking the pan occasionally. The liquid will reduce down to a shiny glaze for the carrots at which point you should remove the pan from the heat and add the parsley.

To finish and serve

1. Spoon a little parsley purée onto each plate and top with a piece of ox cheek or 2. Arrange the carrots alongside and serve the sauce and potato purée at the table.

Ingredients

2 ox cheeks (each cut into 4 with fat removed. Chuck or blade can be substituted).

100g coarse salt

½ tsp ground black pepper

75ml sunflower oil

4 gloves garlic, cracked

1 small onion, peeled and diced

1 small carrot, peeled and diced

1 stick celery, diced

4 inch section of leek, thickly sliced

1 small flat mushroom, diced

2 ripe tomatoes, cut in eighths

500ml red wine

250ml Madeira

1½ litres veal or beef stock

2 bay leaves

A generous sprig of thyme

8 juniper berries lightly crushed

For the garnish

4 medium sized carrots, peeled

60g butter

2 tsp chopped parsley

3 tbsp parsley purée (See Essential Basics section)

4 portions of potato purée (See Essential Basics section)

Slow-cooked Cod, Polenta Chips, Pipérade, Grelot Onions, Red Pepper sauce

Method

For the cod

1. Combine the coarse sea salt with the granulated sugar. Spread a layer of the mixture onto a tray or plate about 1cm thick in the shape of the cod loin. Place the fish on top then cover with another layer of the salt mixture.

2. Place in the fridge for 1½-2 hours then remove and discard the salt and sugar mix. Rinse the cod in plenty of cold water for about an hour then dry well and refrigerate overnight (the cod will remain fresh for 2 days in the fridge once salted).

3. On the day you finish the dish, cut the salted loin into 4 portions and reserve.

For the pipérade

1. Using a pan with a tight-fitting lid, cook the onion and garlic gently in the olive oil with a pinch of salt until the onions are completely soft but still white.

2. Cut the peppers into strips about 3mm thick. Add to the soft onions and continue to cook gently until completely soft. Reserve in a warm place.

For the grelots

1. Trim away any damaged layers from the onions, trim the roots and wash well. Split the onions lengthways into 2 if large – leave whole if small.

2. Heat a non-stick pan large enough to take the onions in a single layer over a moderate to low heat. Add a little olive oil to the pan then place the onions cut side down in the pan to cook. Season with salt then add a few tablespoons of water and cover with a lid. The onions will cook in the steam created; if they are still firm when the water has all gone then add a little more and continue cooking. When tender, remove the lid. The remaining water will evaporate then the onions will begin to fry. They are ready when golden and caramelised. Keep warm until needed.

To finish and serve

1. Heat the oven to 80°C. Place the cod on a tray and brush with a little olive oil.

2. Cook the cod in the oven until the flakes separate easily at the centre (check after 12 minutes but it may take up to 18 minutes depending on the thickness of the fish).

3. Heat the piperade, grelots and the sauce. Deep-fry the polenta chips until golden and crisp. Drain well on absorbent paper.

4. At the last moment, add the roughly-chopped basil to the piperade and place a spoonful on each plate with a piece of the cod on top. Arrange the grelots, polenta and fried parsley around and to finish with the sauce.

Ingredients

600g loin of cod (the thick part of the fillet) trimmed, skin on

3 tbsp olive oil

Coarse sea salt

Granulated sugar

4 portions red pepper sauce (See Essential Basics section)

For the pipérade

4 large basil leaves

2 small red peppers

2 small yellow peppers

½ an onion, peeled and sliced

1 clove of garlic, chopped

3 tbsp olive oil

Pinch of Piment d'Espelette or cayenne, optional

For the garnish

12 leaves of fried flat-leaf parsley (See Essential Basics section)

6 grelot onions or bulbous spring onions

4 portions of polenta chips (See Essential Basics section)

Slow-cooked Fillet of Beef, Ravioli of Ox Cheek, Broccoli Purée, Peanuts, Beer Foam

Serves 4

Ingredients

2 x 8oz tournados of beef fillet

1 clove of garlic

1 sprig of thyme

75g of butter

4 portions red wine sauce (See Essential Basics section)

2 tbsp vegetable oil

Ravioli of Ox Cheek (See Essential Basics section)

For the garnish

1 large or 2 small heads of broccoli

2 tsp spicy peanuts, chopped (See Essential Basics section)

75g unsalted butter

For the beer foam

1 x 500ml bottle Bathams beer or your preferred local beer

250ml water

50g sugar

10g salt

9g soya lecithin (available from health food shops)

Method

For the beef

1. Season the steaks with salt and pepper.
2. Place a heavy frying pan over a high heat and sear the steaks on all sides to give a good colour.
3. Add 75g of butter, a cracked clove of garlic and a sprig of thyme to the pan. Continue cooking, turning the steaks in the butter until they are nicely browned.
4. Place the steaks onto a tray and pour over the butter garlic and thyme. Transfer to a preheated oven (200ºC) and cook to your preference (medium rare will take about 6-8 minutes). Reserve in a warm place.

For the garnish

1. Cut 12 small florets from each head of broccoli and cook them briefly in boiling salted water till just done. Drain and plunge them into iced water. Drain again and reserve in the fridge.
2. Using a sharp knife, cut the green tips from the rest of the broccoli.
3. Cook the tips in boiling salted water until quite soft. Drain and purée in a liquidiser. If necessary add a little water to help blend the mixture and create a smooth and shiny purée.
4. Pass the purée through a fine sieve and keep warm until needed.

For the beer foam

1. Bring the beer to the boil with the sugar. Remove from the heat then add the cold water and blend in the lecithin powder using a hand blender.
2. Keep the foam warm until serving.

To finish and serve

1. Bring a pan of salted water to the boil and drop in the ravioli. Cook until tender – about 4 minutes.
2. Meanwhile warm the sauce and purée. Fry the broccoli in a non-stick pan to brown it slightly. Ensure it is warmed through.
3. Add the ravioli and peanuts to the broccoli pan with 2 teaspoons of butter. Season with salt and pepper.
4. Spoon a little broccoli purée onto each warm plate and spread it a little with 1 stroke of a pastry brush.
5. Cut each steak in 2 and place a piece of beef on top of the purée. Spoon the ravioli, peanut and broccoli mixture onto the plate along with some of the red wine sauce.
6. Finally, aerate the beer foam using a hand blender and spoon a little on top of the beef.

Slow-cooked Fillet of Red Mullet, Heirloom Tomatoes, Tapenade and Baby Courgette

Serves 4

Method

For the red mullet

1. Two hours before you serve, season the fillets lightly with fine salt and return to the fridge for 45 minutes. Rinse the fish in cold water for 5 minutes then drain, pat dry and reserve in the fridge until needed.

For the garnish

1. Slice the tomatoes and arrange on an oven tray, season with salt and black pepper and brush with a little olive oil.

2. Carefully remove the flowers from the courgettes and open each 1 out so that the petals are in a flat sheet, discard the base and stamen.

3. Heat the vegetable oil to around 165°C. Dip the flowers into the tempura batter, allow the excess batter to drain off then fry them until golden and crisp. Drain on absorbent paper and keep the flowers warm.

4. Cut each courgette into 2 barrels and sauté in a little olive oil with the whole peeled garlic clove and a pinch of salt. When they are tender, discard the garlic and keep the courgettes warm.

To finish and serve

1. Heat the oven to 80°C. Brush the fillets with olive oil and place in the oven on a metal tray. Put the tray of tomatoes in the oven.

2. Check the mullet after around 8 minutes. When cooked it will feel firm and the flakes will separate easily. Return the fish to the oven for a few minutes if necessary.

3. Meanwhile brush a ribbon of tapenade across each plate using a pastry brush. Arrange the tomato slices around with the mullet fillets on top. Place the courgettes and courgette flowers in and around, finish with the basil leaves and a drizzle of olive oil.

Ingredients

8 small fillets of red mullet (around 75g each, trimmed and bones removed)

A good pinch of fine salt

A little extra virgin olive oil

3 tbsp black olive tapenade (See Essential Basics section)

For the garnish

4 baby courgettes with flowers attached

A selection of heirloom tomatoes of different colours, shapes and sizes to give about 5 slices per person

A few sprigs of basil

2 tbsp extra virgin olive oil

Salt and black pepper

2 tbsp tempura batter (See Essential Basics section)

Vegetable oil for deep frying

1 clove of garlic, peeled

Red mullet is prized for its delicate flesh and refined flavour and the heirloom tomatoes really help lift this dish without overpowering it.

Sticky Glazed Spare Ribs

Serves 6 as a starter or 4 as a main course

Ingredients

2 racks of pork ribs
100ml sunflower oil
4 tbsp smoked salt
2 tbsp Espelette pepper
or chilli flakes
2 tsp crushed dried rosemary
2 tsp ground black pepper
1 tsp ground cumin
4 tsp smoked paprika

For the glaze

50g sunflower oil
3 cloves garlic, crushed
400ml veal demi-glace (See
Essential Basics section)
400ml ketchup
100ml honey or maple syrup
1 dstsp Worcestershire sauce
100g soft brown sugar
100ml sherry vinegar

Method

For the glaze

1. Heat the sunflower oil over moderate heat. Add the garlic and fry briefly until beginning to colour. Add the honey to stop the garlic cooking any further followed by all the other ingredients.

2. Simmer gently, stirring often until the glaze becomes sticky. Keep warm until needed.

To cook the ribs

1. Trim away any unsightly parts from the racks of ribs.

2. Combine all of the salt, spices and rosemary in a bowl and rub over both sides of the racks, working in well.

3. Set the oven to 220°C.

4. Coat the ribs with sunflower oil and roast for around 40 minutes or until nicely browned and tender between the bones.

5. Remove from the oven and brush thickly with the glaze then return to the oven for 5-6 minutes. Repeat the glaze and bake process once more and allow to cool a little before serving and cutting the ribs.

*An easy one to cook, and serve.
My kids love this for sunday lunch.*

Baked Egg Custard Tart with Nutmeg

Serves 8-10 people (24cm tart case)

Method

1. Roll the pastry out to the thickness of a 2 pence piece and line the tart tin with it (use a tin with a loose base to make it easy to remove the tart later). Allow any excess pastry to hang over the edge of the tin to be trimmed after baking.

2. Chill the pastry for 20 minutes before baking.

3. Line the chilled tart base with baking parchment and fill with baking beans. Bake at 175°C for around 15 minutes then remove the paper and beans and continue baking until the base is golden and crisp at the centre.

4. Brush the hot tart base with the beaten egg and return to the oven for 3-4 minutes to set the egg. This helps to keep the tart crisp. Set aside while you make the filling. Reduce the oven temperature to 125°C.

5. Heat the cream while you whisk together the yolks and sugar. Pour the boiling cream onto the yolks and sugar, whisking continuously. Pass the custard through a fine sieve into a jug.

6. Pour the custard into the cooked pastry case and place in the oven. Once ready to bake, grate the nutmeg liberally over the surface. Shut the oven door and bake for around 30 minutes or until just set but has a slight wobble. Remove from the oven and cool before cutting.

Ingredients

300g sweet pastry (See Essential Basics section)

1 egg, beaten

550ml whipping cream

80g caster sugar

8 egg yolks

Fresh nutmeg and a fine grater

As English as can be - don't forget the wobble.

163

Sherry Trifle

Ingredients

For the sponge

3 large eggs at room temperature
90g caster sugar
90g plain flour, sifted
50g unsalted butter,
melted and cooled

For the syrup

100g caster sugar
125ml water
1 strip of orange zest
1 strip of lemon zest
Squeeze of lemon juice
100ml sweet sherry, or to taste

For the custard

300ml milk
300ml whipping cream
1 vanilla pod, split
8 egg yolks
100g caster sugar
40g custard powder

For the raspberry mixture

6 tbsp good quality raspberry jam
125g fresh raspberries,
plus a few for decoration

For the cream

1 tbsp flaked almonds, toasted
500ml whipping cream
75g caster sugar
Seeds scraped from
half a vanilla pod

Method

For the sponge

1. Whisk the eggs with the sugar in a large bowl until you have a thick pale foam which will just hold its shape.

2. Fold in the flour and melted butter, then pour the mixture into a Swiss roll tin or similar which has been greased and lined with baking parchment. Aim for a layer about an inch deep.

3. Bake in an oven pre-heated to 180°C for 10-12 minutes or until it springs back when pressed lightly at the centre.

4. Turn the sponge out on a wire rack to cool.

For the syrup

1. Bring the sugar, water and zests to the boil and remove from the heat once the sugar has dissolved.

2. Cool the syrup and then add the sherry and lemon juice.

For the custard

1. Bring the milk, cream, and vanilla to the boil.

2. Meanwhile, whisk the sugar, egg yolks, and custard powder together.

3. Whisk the boiling milk mixture onto the yolks mixture, and return to the pan.

4. Cook over a moderate heat, stirring at all times until the mixture has bubbled for about a minute.

5. Pass the mixture through a fine sieve, cover with cling film, and keep warm.

For the raspberry mixture

1. Place the jam and raspberries in a bowl and combine with a fork, crushing the raspberries a little as you go.

For the topping and to assemble the trifle

1. The trifle can be assembled in either 8 small glasses, or a large bowl.

2. Cut the cooled sponge into 2cm squares, and place a layer in the base of your glasses or bowl.

3. Spoon over enough sherry syrup to moisten the sponge well.

4. Top the sponge with a layer of raspberry mixture, followed by a layer of warm vanilla custard. Allow the custard layer to cool completely in the fridge.

5. Meanwhile, whip the cream with the caster sugar and vanilla to give a soft peak consistency.

6. When the custard layer is chilled, spoon the vanilla cream on the top to fill the glasses or bowl.

7. Decorate the top with a few flaked almonds and fresh raspberries.

Black Forest in a glass

Serves 4 people

Method

For the chocolate sponge

1. Heat the oven to 175°C and line a 15cm cake tin with baking parchment.
2. Whisk the eggs and sugar until they form a thick sabayon. Sift the cocoa powder and flour together.
3. Fold the flour into the sabayon, adding the butter when halfway through the process. Continue mixing until the mixture is smooth.
4. Pour the batter into a lined tin and bake for around 20 minutes or until a skewer comes out clean when inserted into the centre.
5. Cool the cake on a rack.
6. When cool, cut the cake into chunky cubes and reserve.

For the cherry compote

1. Place the cornflour in a small bowl and add 3 tablespoons of the cherry juice and mix into a paste.
2. Heat the rest of the cherry juice with the sugar and orange zest. When boiling, whisk in the cornflour solution off the heat then return to the boil for a minute or so until thickened.
3. Stir in the cherries then pour the whole mixture into a bowl. Add the kirsch and leave to cool.

For the cream

1. Whip the cream with the sugar and vanilla seeds to form soft peaks. Reserve in the fridge.

For the soaking syrup

1. Bring the sugar and water to the boil and remove from the heat once the sugar is dissolved. When cooled, add the kirsch to taste.

To assemble and finish

1. Place a layer of chocolate sponge cubes in the bottom of 4 glasses (or a large bowl). Spoon over a little kirsch syrup to moisten the sponge then top with a layer of cherry compote.
2. Finally, spoon the cream on top.
3. If you wish, shave some chocolate from a bar using a potato peeler and sprinkle on top of the cream.

Ingredients

For the chocolate sponge

4 eggs
120g sugar
100g flour
25g cocoa powder
25g melted butter at room temperature

For the cherry compote

1 tin of black cherries in juice
1 strip of orange zest
1 tbsp caster sugar
2 tbsp kirsch
2 tbsp cornflour

For the soaking syrup

100ml water
100ml sugar
2 tbsp kirsch, or to your taste

For the cream

300ml whipping cream
30g caster sugar
The seeds scraped from ½ vanilla pod

Chai Pannacotta, Mango Compote and Coconut Sorbet

Serves 8

Method

For the pannacotta

1. Heat a pan large enough for the cream and milk over a moderate heat. Toast the cinnamon and cardamon in the dry pan briefly until they become fragrant.

2. Add the cream, milk, sugar and bay leaves. Bring to the boil and add the tea. Remove from the heat. Allow the tea and spices to infuse until you are happy with the strength of flavour (about 6 or 8 minutes or longer if using tea bags).

3. Pass the warm mixture through muslin or a fine sieve into a jug then pour into 8 metal dariole moulds of about 80ml capacity. Chill in the fridge to set.

For the mango compote and coconut biscuits

1. Peel the mango and dice the flesh. Add sugar, lime juice and zest to taste then reserve.

2. Place all the ingredients for the biscuit mix in the bowl of a food processor and mix to a paste. Work in the melted butter for a few seconds until smooth.

3. Spoon some of the mixture onto baking parchment and spread thinly with a palette knife.

4. Bake at 170°C until pale golden brown and crisp when cooled. Break the cooled biscuit into shards ready to garnish the pannacotta.

To serve

1. When the pannacotta are set, dip each mould briefly into hot water and slip them out, 1 onto each plate.

2. Spoon a little mango compote next to each with some coconut shavings and a scoop of coconut sorbet. Finish with a piece of coconut biscuit.

Ingredients

For the pannacotta

15g cassia bark or cinnamon, broken into pieces

10g cardamon pods, split

10g Indian bay leaves (or European)

10g finely grated fresh ginger

600ml whipping cream

150ml milk

150g sugar

4 tsp loose tea (or 4 tea bags)

3 leaves gelatine (soaked in cold water for 10 minutes then drained well)

For the mango compote

2 or 3 mangoes (Indian Alfonso mangoes are best)

A little icing sugar

A little finely grated lime zest and juice

1 recipe of coconut sorbet (See page 172)

A few shavings from a fresh coconut for garnish

For the coconut biscuit

75g dessicated coconut

75g icing sugar

25g flour

60g egg white

50g butter, melted

I have my wife Nibedita to thank for the Indian influence in this dish. I also have to thank her for putting up with me during the time it took to do this book!

Chocolate Baked Alaska

Method

For the ice-cream

1. Heat the cream, milk and cocoa powder together. Whisk the yolks with the sugar. When the cream mixture starts to simmer, whisk it onto the yolks then return to the pan.

2. Cook over a gentle heat, stirring constantly until the mixture coats the back of the spoon.

3. Remove from the heat and stir in the chopped chocolate until completely melted and smooth. Pass through a fine sieve and churn in an ice-cream machine.

4. When churned you will need to set the ice-cream in small domed containers or ramekins which have been lined with a double layer of cling film. They should be of 120-150ml capacity for an individual serving. Keep the filled domes or ramekins in the freezer until you are ready for the next stage.

For the sponge cake base

1. Whisk the eggs and sugar until they are pale and foamy. Fold in the flour and melted butter then pour the mixture onto a tray lined with baking parchment.

2. Spread with a spatula to about 5mm thick and bake at 190°C for 7-10 minutes or until the surface springs back when pressed lightly. Cool on a wire rack, when cool remove the parchment.

3. Cut the sponge into discs the same size as your ice-cream moulds then press a disc onto the ice-cream. This will form an insulating base when the ice-cream is in the oven.

For the Italian meringue

1. Before making the meringue turn the moulded ice-creams out onto their bases on a parchment lined oven tray leaving a few inches space inbetween. Carefully remove the cling film and return to the freezer.

2. Mix the 250g of sugar with the water and boil to dissolve then cook to 121°C, testing with a sugar thermometer.

3. When the sugar has been cooking for a few minutes begin whisking the egg whites with the 20g sugar to stiff peaks.

4. When the sugar reaches 121°C pour it onto the whisking egg whites in a steady stream then continue whisking until cold.

5. Spoon the meringue into a piping bag fitted with ½cm star nozzle.

6. Take the tray of chocolate ice-cream from the freezer and pipe the meringue onto each dome. Ensure there are no gaps in the meringue as the heat of the oven will penetrate and melt the ice-cream.

7. When all domes are coated return the whole tray back to the freezer until ready to bake.

To finish and serve

1. Heat your oven to 220°C place the frozen Alaskas in the oven for 4-6 minutes or until golden brown.

2. Serve immediately and accompany with a raspberry coulis. (See Essential Basics section).

Note: A good quality shop-bought ice-cream will suffice if you don't have an ice-cream machine.

Note: These can be prepared until this stage up to 3 days before then stored in the freezer until needed.

Ingredients

Chocolate ice-cream

180g chocolate (70% cocoa solids), chopped

6 egg yolks

100g caster sugar

450ml whole milk

50ml cream

1 tbsp cocoa powder

Italian meringue

125ml egg white

20g sugar

250g caster sugar

100ml water

Sponge cake base

2 eggs

60g caster sugar

60g plain flour, sieved

20g melted butter

Chocolate Soufflé and Coconut Sorbet

Serves 4

Ingredients

For the soufflé

30g egg yolk

150ml milk

10g cornflour

150g 70% plain chocolate, melted (we recommend Valrhona, French chocolatiers)

100g egg whites

40g sugar

60g soft butter and a little caster sugar for the ramekins

For the sorbet

120ml water

120g sugar

400g coconut milk

Method

Note: This soufflé recipe is very useful as you can make them a day or 2 in advance, freeze them uncooked in their ramekins then simply bake from the freezer allowing 2 minutes extra in the oven.

For the sorbet

1. Bring the water and sugar to the boil, making sure all the sugar is dissolved.
2. Mix the coconut milk with the sugar syrup and when cooled churn in an ice-cream maker.
3. Reserve in the freezer when ready.

For the soufflé

1. Brush the inside of your ramekins with the soft butter then dust with caster sugar. Tip out the excess.
2. Mix the cornflour with 2 tablespoons of the milk.
3. Bring the rest of the milk to the boil then whisk in the cornflour mixture.
4. When the mixture has boiled for 30 seconds-1 minute, remove it from the heat, whisk in the egg yolk followed by the chocolate.
5. The mixture should be smooth and shiny.
6. Keep the mixture slightly warm but not hot.
7. Whisk the egg whites until they begin to become foamy, add the sugar and continue whisking until you have a smooth shiny meringue which will hold its own shape.
8. Add a quarter of the whites to the soufflé base and whisk. Add half of the remaining whites and fold in gently using a spatula. When half mixed add the remaining whites and continue to fold together until completely smooth with no white flecks.
9. Spoon the mixture into the ramekins.
10. If you are baking the soufflés straight away, they will need around 7-8 minutes at 180°C. They can be refrigerated for up to 4 hours but allow an extra minute or so in the oven.

To serve

1. Serve the soufflés hot from the oven with the coconut sorbet alongside.

Soufflé... the king of all puddings. Light, fluffy and in this case yummy and chocolatey with a dollop of coconut sorbet - a marriage made in heaven.

Chocolate Tart, Caramel Pecans with Banana and Lime Ice-cream

Serves 4

Ingredients

For the chocolate sable base

100g soft unsalted butter

20g icing sugar

35g ground almonds

Pinch salt

1 egg, beaten

130g plain flour

16g cocoa powder

Chocolate tart filling

285g chocolate (70% cocoa solids), melted

325ml double cream

75g soft butter

Caramel pecans

75g caster sugar

125g double cream

100g pecans, lighted toasted

Banana and lime ice-cream

250ml milk

250ml whipping cream

80g egg yolk (approximately 4 yolks)

175g caster sugar

2 lime zests grated and juice squeezed

5 bananas

75g lime juice

Method

Note: Use a loose bottomed tart tin as it will make removing the tart much easier.

For the sable base

1. Beat together the butter, icing sugar, ground almonds and salt until pale in colour, and then add the egg.

2. Sift the flour and cocoa powder together and add to the butter mixture. Bring the mixture together and when smooth wrap in cling film and refrigerate until completely firm (about 2 hours).

3. When the sable mix is thoroughly chilled, roll it on a lightly floured surface to about the thickness of a pound coin, then cut it to fit your tart tin or tray. Chill for 30 minutes.

4. Prick the sable base with a fork and cover with baking parchment topped with a layer of baking beans or rice to stop the base from rising in the oven.

5. Bake at 175°C for 15 minutes then remove the beans and parchment and bake for a further 5-10 minutes or until crisp.

6. Reserve the base in the tin while you make the filling.

Note: This mixture can be made the day before and kept in the fridge and any extra can be frozen for upto 1 month.

For the chocolate filling

1. Check the temperature of the melted chocolate; it should feel warm but not too hot (35-40°C).

2. Heat the cream in a pan to around the same temperature.

3. Using a spatula, gradually incorporate the cream into the chocolate to give a smooth, shiny and supple mixture, and then mix in the butter. The warmth of the chocolate and cream should melt the butter into the mixture.

4. Pour the chocolate mixture onto the cooled base and tap lightly to level it out. Refrigerate for at least 30 minutes to set the tart.

For the banana and lime ice-cream

1. Heat the milk and whipping cream to boiling point. In the meantime, whisk together the yolks, sugar and lime zest.

2. Whisk the boiling milk and cream onto the yolk mixture and return to the pan and cook gently stirring all the time until the mixture thickens slightly (85°C approx).

3. Remove from the heat and cool quickly. Meanwhile, slice the bananas and mix with the lime juice. When the ice cream base is cold, place it, the bananas and lime in a liquidiser jug and process for 2-3 minutes. Pass through a fine sieve and churn in an ice-cream maker. Reserve in the freezer when ready.

For the caramel pecans

1. Cook the sugar in a largish pan with just enough water to dissolve it, continue cooking until the sugar is a rich caramel colour. Reduce the heat and add a third of the cream. The caramel will splutter so be careful.

2. When the first addition has combined with the caramel, add the rest of the cream. Stir to combine and cook to a glossy caramel (about 106°C) then remove from the heat.

3. Stir in the pecans and keep warm.

To finish and serve

1. Run a small knife around the edge of the tart tin to release the filling from the edge, and then lift out the tart ready for cutting.

2. Dip your knife into hot water for a clean edge and cut portions of the tart as you wish.

3. Top with the caramel pecans and a scoop of ice-cream alongside.

Hot Churros, Coffee Ice-Cream, Kahlua Mascarpone, Espresso Granite and Frothy Milk

Serves 4

Method

For the churros mixture

1. Bring the water and butter to the boil in a saucepan over moderate heat. When the mixture begins to boil, immediately add the flour, salt and sugar and mix quickly with a wooden spoon until smooth.
2. Return the pan to the heat and continue stirring while the mixture cooks and dries a little, leaving a coating around the inside of the pan. About 5 or 6 minutes should do it.
3. Tip the mixture into the bowl of an electric mixer and turn the mixer onto its lowest speed.
4. After about 5 minutes of mixing the temperature will have dropped enough to add the eggs. Do this gradually and allow each addition to combine thoroughly before adding the next.
5. When all the egg is incorporated, spoon the mixture into a piping bag filled with a 1cm star shaped nozzle. Reserve until needed.

For the Kahlua mascarpone

1. Whip the cream with the sugar and Kahlua to soft peaks.
2. Beat the mascarpone to soften a little then fold the 2 mixtures together and keep in the fridge. If the mixture softens too much before you use it then rewhisk to firm it a little.

For the coffee ice-cream

1. Bring the milk, cream and coffee beans to the boil. Meanwhile, whisk the yolks and sugar together.
2. When the milk mixture boils, whisk it onto the yolks then return the whole back to the pan and stir over a low heat until slightly thickened (about 85°C).
3. Remove from the heat and pass through a sieve into a clean bowl. If you prefer a stronger coffee flavour leave the coffee beans in the mixture and strain when cold.
4. Churn in an ice-cream maker and keep in the freezer until needed.

For the espresso granite

1. Dissolve the sugar in 1 cup of espresso over a low heat then combine the rest of the coffee and freeze the mixture in a bowl or tray.
2. When frozen crush to a coarse texture with the back of a fork and return to the freezer until needed.

To serve and finish

1. Heat the sunflower oil to 170°C. Cut pieces of baking parchment about 10cm square and pipe ovals of churros mixture onto each square.
2. Gently lower the paper squares into the oil, the churros will separate from the paper allowing you to lift the paper out of the oil to discard it.
3. Cook the churros 2 or 3 at a time turning them when the first side is golden brown. Drain them on kitchen towel when cooked and toss in caster sugar before serving.
4. Spoon a little mascarpone mixture into each of 4 glasses or small bowls, top with a spoonful of the granite and ice-cream. Finally, froth the semi-skimmed milk as if making a cappuccino and spoon over.
5. Serve with the hot churros.
6. Alternatively, serve the churros with hot chocolate sauce or even with a mug of hot chocolate.

Ingredients

For the churros mixture

150g water

100g butter, unsalted

135g plain flour

15g sugar

Pinch salt

2 eggs, beaten

1 litre sunflower oil to fry the churros

For the Kahlua Mascarpone

250g mascarpone

100g double cream

50g caster sugar

Kahlua Liqueur to taste (or Tia Maria)

For the Coffee Ice-Cream

250ml milk

175ml whipping cream

100g sugar

100g egg yolk

40g crushed coffee beans (or 2-3 tsp coffee granules)

For the espresso granite

4 espresso cups full of strong espresso coffee

1 espresso cup of caster sugar

For the milk froth

250ml UHT semi-skimmed milk

You will need a milk frothing device or a hand blender

Lemon Cake

Serves 4

Ingredients

3 large eggs
175g caster sugar
Pinch of salt
75g double cream
140g self raising flour
50g unsalted butter, melted
Finely grazed zest of 2 lemons
2 tbsp rum, optional

For the lemon syrup

100g sugar
100g water
40g lemon juice

For the lemon glaze

100g icing sugar
30ml lemon juice, approximately

Method

1. Line a 24cm cake tin with baking parchment and set aside. Heat the oven to 180°C.
2. Whisk the eggs and sugar together until foamy. Stir in the flour followed by the zest, cream, butter and rum if using.
3. Pour into the tin and bake for 10 minutes before reducing the heat to 170°C.
4. Continue baking for around 15-20 minutes or until a skewer can be inserted and pulled out clean. Remove from the oven.

For the lemon syrup

1. Boil the sugar and water together to dissolve. Cool then add the lemon juice.
2. Spoon some of the syrup over the cake and allow to soak in. Repeat every 5-10 minutes until you are happy that your cake is moist enough. You may have some syrup left.

To serve and finish

1. Whisk the icing sugar and lemon juice until smooth to give a slightly runny consistency.
2. Place the cooled cake on a wire rack over an oven tray. Pour over the icing and spread to coat the top and sides of the cake evenly.
3. Immediately place the cake in the oven at 220°C for around 20-30 seconds then remove and cool completely.
4. Store in an airtight box until serving or upto 3 days.

After all that cooking sit down, have a cup of tea, and cut yourself a slice.

Mandarin and Lemon Thyme Sorbet, Almond Meringues, Chocolate Cream and Crushed Shortbread

Serves 4

Method

For the sorbet

1. Heat the water, half the mandarin juice, thyme and mandarin zest to dissolve the sugar. Mix the milk powder with the glucose powder and whisk into the liquid, remove from the heat.
2. Add the remaining mandarin juice and leave the mixture to cool and take on the flavour of the thyme. Pass through a sieve and churn the sorbet in an ice-cream machine then store in the freezer until needed.

For the almond meringues

1. Combine the 2 sugars and mix thoroughly.
2. Whisk the egg whites with the lemon juice, salt and 1 tablespoon of the sugar until they begin to foam. Continue whisking and gradually adding the sugar to give a stiff and shiny meringue.
3. Spoon the meringue into a piping bag fitted with a 5mm plain nozzle and pipe the mixture onto baking parchment on a baking tray. We pipe ours into sticks about 6cm long but you can vary the shape as you wish.
4. Sprinkle the piped meringues with the almond flakes and dry them in a warm oven (about 90°C) until completely crisp but still white.
5. Store in an airtight tub until needed.

For the chocolate cream

1. Melt the chocolate over hot water or in the microwave on low power. The chocolate should be at about 35°C.
2. Heat the cream and milk in a medium saucepan. Meanwhile, whisk together the yolks and sugar. When the cream mixture boils, whisk it onto the yolks and sugar. Return to the pan and cook, stirring at all times until the mixture has thickened slightly (85°C).
3. Strain the custard through a sieve into a jug.
4. Using a spatula, gradually incorporate the warm custard into the chocolate to give a smooth shiny mixture. For an extra smooth and silky texture, mix the cream in a liquidiser or with a hand blender for a minute.
5. Spoon the cream into a piping bag with a 1cm nozzle and chill in the fridge for 3 hours minimum or upto 2 days.

For the crushed shortbread

1. Mix the flour, butter and sugar together gently to give a smooth dough. Press into a parchment lined baking sheet to a thickness of a pound coin using your hands with a dusting of flour as necessary. Chill in the fridge for 30 minutes then bake at 175°C for about 15 minutes or until golden and cooked through. Remove from the oven and cool on a rack.
2. When cool and crisp, crush enough shortbread for 4 servings in a bowl with the back of a fork to give a light sandy texture.
3. Reserve the shortbread in an airtight tub until needed.

To finish and serve the dish

1. Place a round or oblong pastry cutter on each plate and inside each press a heaped tablespoon of crushed shortbread. Smooth flat with the back of the spoon and gently remove the rings.
2. Pipe 2 or 3 small domes of chocolate cream on each plate. Add a few mandarin segments then a scoop of sorbet. Finally, finish with 2 or 3 almond meringues and serve immediately.

Ingredients

For the sorbet

100ml water
500ml mandarin juice
Zest of 2 mandarins, grated
10g milk powder
50g glucose powder (available from health food shops)
100g caster sugar
4 sprigs of fresh lemon thyme

For the almond meringues

90g egg whites (about 3)
65g caster sugar
65g icing sugar, sifted
Few drops of lemon juice
Small pinch of salt
2 tbsp toasted almond flakes

For the chocolate cream

130g whipping cream
130g milk
50g egg yolks
25g caster sugar
140g Valrhona macae chocolate (or similar with 62% chocolate cocoa solids)

For the crushed shortbread

150g plain flour
100g unsalted butter, softened
50g caster sugar

To garnish the dish

4 sprigs lemon thyme
2 tbsp fresh mandarin segments

Mini Strawberry and Pistachio Cakes, Crème de Fraise Jelly and Lemon Sorbet

Serves 4

Ingredients

For the cakes

95g ground almonds

110g icing sugar

125g egg whites (about 4)

40g caster sugar

2 tsp pistachio oil (or vegetable oil)

20g green pistachio, finely chopped or powdered in a food processor

For the pastry cream

250ml milk

2 egg yolks

50g caster sugar

12g custard powder

12g plain flour

25g green pistachios, finely chopped or powdered (optional)

For the lemon sherbet

570ml milk

210g sugar

Grated zest and juice of 3 lemons

For the strawberry jelly

140ml strawberry syrup (See Essential Basics section)

10ml strawberry liqueur (crème de fraise)

1 leaf gelatine (soaked in cold water for 10 minutes then drained well)

To serve

1 punnet ripe strawberries

Method

For the pistachio cakes

1. Sift together the ground almonds and icing sugar. Whisk the whites and sugar to stiff peaks then fold in the almond mixture followed by the pistachio oil and pistachio powder.

2. Spoon the mixture into 4 inch cake rings which have been previously buttered and coated with caster sugar and placed on a tray lined with baking parchment. The mixture should be about a 1cm deep in each ring.

3. Bake at 165°C until risen and set but still moist at the centre (about 12-15 minutes).

4. Cool on a cake rack until needed.

For the pastry cream

1. Heat the milk in a medium pan, meanwhile whisk together the yolks and sugar then add the flour and custard powder and whisk again until smooth.

2. When the milk begins to boil, whisk it onto the yolk mixture then return the whole to the pan and cook over a moderate heat, stirring constantly until bubbling and thickened.

3. Pour the pastry cream into a bowl and stir in the pistachios if you opt for them – they really add an extra kick of pistachio to the dish. Cover the bowl with cling film and allow to cool.

For the lemon sherbet

1. Bring the milk, sugar and zest to the boil then add the lemon juice. Pass the mixture through a fine sieve. Cool the mixture then churn in an ice-cream machine and store in the freezer until needed.

For the strawberry jelly

1. Heat half of the strawberry syrup then stir in the drained gelatine followed by the strawberry liqueur.

2. Pass the mixture through a fine sieve and mix with the remainder of the strawberry syrup.

3. Set the jelly in a shallow tray lined with cling film in the fridge. It should take about 2 hours to set after which you can cut it into cubes and return to the fridge until needed.

To finish and serve

1. Wash and quarter the strawberries.

2. Remove each mini cake carefully from each ring, spoon a little crème patisserie into the centre of each cake and arrange the strawberries and jelly cubes on top with a scoop of the sherbet alongside.

Pain Perdu with Apples and Blackberries, Brioche French Toast

Serves 4

Ingredients

4 thick slices of brioche
75g sugar to caramelise the brioche
50g butter

For the custard

300g whipping cream
25g caster sugar
3 eggs yolks
½ a vanilla pod, seeds scraped and pod reserved

For the garnish

150g mascarpone
2 dessert apples, peeled, cored, and cut into thick wedges
The reserved vanilla pod
125g blackberries
2 tbsp caster sugar
1 tbsp butter
1 tbsp Calvados, optional or apple juice

Method

Note: A traditional French dessert with a very English combination.

To soak the brioche

1. Whisk together the cream, yolks, sugar and vanilla seeds.

2. Place the brioche slices in a tray deep enough to hold them and the custard. Pour over the custard and soak for about 10 minutes, turning after 5 minutes. Drain the slices and reserve on a tray until you are ready to cook them.

To cook the fruit

1. Heat a non-stick pan large enough to take the apple wedges in 1 layer. Add the sugar, butter, vanilla pod, Calvados or apple juice to the pan with the apples. Cook steadily, turning occasionally for 6-8 minutes or until the apples are just tender then add the blackberries and remove to a warm place. The blackberries should soften a little but not burst too much.

To cook the pain perdu and finish the dish

1. In a non-stick pan, heat the 50g of butter with the 75g of sugar until it begins to caramelise. Lay the brioche slices in the pan and cook over a moderate heat until nicely browned. Turn and repeat on the second side then remove to a clean tray. Try not to overcook the centre – it should remain moist.

2. When the caramel has set a little, place a finished pain perdu on each plate, spoon the warm apples and blackberries on top and finish with a spoonful of mascarpone.

I prepare this with students in our cookery school, it has the wow factor every time.

Peach, Cherry and Amaretti Crumble

Serves 6

Method

For the crumble

1. Rub the butter into the flour to form a coarse breadcrumb texture then add the sugar.
2. Spread the mixture on an oven tray in an even layer and bake at 170°C for around 15 minutes or until golden. You may need to stir and turn a little after 10 minutes. The crumble should become crisp when cooled a little.
3. When cool enough to handle, mix in the crushed amaretti biscuits and set the crumble to 1 side. The crumble can be prepared to this stage up to 2 days ahead if stored in an airtight container.

For the fruit

1. Cut the peaches in half and remove the stones. Cut each half into chunky wedges.
2. Scatter the peaches and cherries across a large oven tray and dredge with caster sugar. Taste the raw fruit and adjust the quantity of sugar accordingly. You can add more later, but will need some to get the fruit juices flowing.
3. Bake the fruit at 170°C until softened and a little juicy. Tip from the tray into a crumble dish. If excessively juicy, spoon a little out.
4. Top with the crumble mixture and warm for 6-8 minutes in the oven.
5. Serve with either custard, cream, crème frâiche or ice-cream.

Ingredients

For the crumble

100g plain flour

65g unsalted butter

35g sugar

200g Amaretti biscuits, crushed lightly

For the fruit

600g firm peaches

300g cherries, stoned

25g-75g sugar depending on the sweetness of the fruit

2 tbsp cherry brandy/Kirsch or Peche de Vigre, optional

Rhubarb in the Spring, Apple in the Autumn and Winter, but this one's definitely a Summer dish.

Raspberry and Pistachio Trifle

Ingredients

For the raspberry jelly

275g of raspberry syrup (See Essential Basics section)

1½ leaves of gelatine soaked in cold water for 10 minutes, then drained and squeezed dry

For the pistachio sponge

60g of green pistachios ground to a powder

85g of icing sugar

40g plain flour

85g soft butter

30g egg yolk

20g whole egg

45g egg whites

40ml milk

20g caster sugar

For the soaking syrup

100ml water

100g sugar

(boiled together and cooled)

For the mascarpone cream

150g mascarpone

75ml whipping cream

Seeds from ½ a vanilla pod

30g of caster sugar

For the meringue

90g egg whites (roughly 3)

65g caster sugar

65g icing sugar

A few drops of lemon juice

Small pinch salt

For the raspberry foam

400g raspberry coulis (See Essential Basics section)

100g water

100g sugar

3 leaves of gelatine (soaked in cold water for 10 minutes, then drained and squeezed dry)

Method

For the raspberry jelly

1. Heat half the syrup over a low heat until hot, stir in the gelatine to dissolve and then mix with the other half of the syrup. Pour the warm jelly into your chosen glasses to a depth of about 1-2cm, depending on the shape. Place in the fridge to set for at least 1 hour.

For the pistachio sponge cake

1. Beat the pistachios, icing sugar, flour and soft butter together until smooth, and then add the egg, yolk and milk to the mixture.

2. Whisk the egg whites with the sugar to firm peaks then fold into the mixture in 3 additions.

3. Spread the cake batter onto a baking tray lined with parchment paper to roughly 1cm thick.

4. Bake at 170°C for 10-15 minutes or until the cake springs back when pressed lightly at the centre.

5. Remove from the oven and cool on a wire rack.

6. Brush the cake with a little of the syrup.

7. When cool cut into small squares and reserve.

For the mascarpone cream

1. Whip the cream with the sugar and vanilla seeds until it holds its shape but is not too firm.

2. Beat the mascarpone to slacken it a little then fold in the whipped cream and reserve in the fridge.

For the meringue drops

1. Whisk the whites with 1 tablespoon of the sugar until they begin to foam, then continue whisking and adding the sugar gradually until you have a shiny firm meringue.

2. Spoon the meringue into a piping bag fitted with a 5mm nozzle. Release small drops onto an oven tray lined with baking parchment.

3. Place the meringue in a low oven (90°C) to dry for around 4 hours or until crisp but still white.

4. Reserve in an air tight tin.

Note: This recipe will yield more than is needed for 4 people. Any extra will keep perfectly for 2-3 weeks in an airtight container.

For the raspberry foam

1. Heat the water and sugar until the sugar has dissolved. Stir in the gelatine and when completely melted add half the coulis to the pan but do not heat it any further; the warmth from the pan will be sufficient.

2. Pour the contents of the pan through a sieve into the remaining coulis and stir to combine. Chill the mixture. After about an hour it will set lightly.

3. Beat the mixture to slacken it a little then pour into a cream whipping canister. Screw the lid on firmly and charge the canister with 2 gas cartridges then reserve in the fridge.

To finish and serve

1. Remove the glasses of jelly from the fridge and spoon a generous layer of mascarpone cream onto the jelly. Follow this with a layer of the moist pistachio cake and some of the raspberries.

2. Shake the canister vigorously then top each glass with foam and finish with meringue drops.

Raspberry Sable Tart

Ingredients

For the sable base

60g egg yolk

120g caster sugar

120g butter (at room temperature)

190g plain flour

11g baking powder

For the creamy raspberry mixture

100g raspberry coulis (See Essential Basics section), save a little extra for the plate

30g egg yolk

35g egg

30g sugar

1½g gelatine (soaked in cold water for 10 minutes and squeezed dry)

35g unsalted butter, softened

For the vanilla ice-cream

250ml milk

175ml double cream

1 vanilla pod, split and deseeded

100g sugar

100g yolks

To serve

2 punnets fresh raspberries

Method

Note: All the elements of this dish can be prepared the day before and assembled before serving.

For the sable

1. Whisk the sugar and yolks until pale then mix in the soft butter.
2. Sift the flour and baking powder together then stir into the mix to give a smooth, soft dough.
3. Chill the dough for 2-3 hours or until completely set.
4. When thoroughly chilled, roll the dough out between 2 sheets of baking parchment to the thickness of a pound coin.
5. Then chill, or even better, freeze the dough until completely set again (it is easier to handle when frozen).
6. Cut the chilled dough to fit the base of your tart tin or tins. We use a 10cm ring for an individual serving or you could use a large ring and cut a wedge of tart for each person.
7. Bake the sable inside the tart ring or rings at 165°C until risen and golden brown. Cool and remove from the ring.

Creamy raspberry mixture

1. Mix the eggs, yolks, sugar and raspberry purée in a heatproof bowl and place over a pan of simmering water. Whisk the mixture regularly.
2. When the mixture is hot to touch and has thickened, remove from the heat and whisk in the gelatine to dissolve. Allow to cool to blood temperature then whisk in the soft butter. Pass the mixture through a sieve and store, covered, in the fridge.

For the vanilla ice-cream

1. Bring the milk, cream, vanilla pods and seeds to the boil.
2. Meanwhile whisk together the sugar and egg yolks.
3. When boiling, whisk the milk and cream onto the yolks and sugar then return the mixture to the pan.
4. Cook the mix over a low heat, stirring at all times until the mixture thickens slightly (about 85°C). Pass the thickened custard through a sieve and cool.
5. When cool, churn in an ice-cream machine and reserve in the freezer.

To finish and serve

1. Spread a little of the raspberry cream onto each baked sable base and top with the raspberries.
2. Spoon a little raspberry purée onto each plate and place a tart and a scoop of ice cream alongside.

Note: A shot of raspberry liqueur adds a little something to the raspberry cream.

To get the fullest flavour from the caramelised apple, serve it at room temperature.

Tarte Tatin in a glass

Serves 4

Method

For the caramelised apple compote

1. Cut both types of apple into chunky pieces roughly 1cm square.
2. Place the sugar into a pan (ensure it's big enough to accommodate the apples later) with the water and boil to dissolve. Continue cooking the syrup until it begins to caramelise, swirling the pan carefully so that the caramel cooks evenly.
3. The caramel should be a rich amber brown colour but not so dark that the taste will be bitter – trust your judgement on timing.
4. When you are happy with the caramel, carefully add the apples, reduce the heat a little and stir to combine. Be careful as the mix will splutter and bubble at first.
5. Cook the mixture gently until the Bramley apples have melted down and the dessert apples are tender.
6. Remove from the heat and add the calvados. Cool to room temperature.

Note: Apples can vary in sweetness so taste the finished compote and add a little caster sugar if you feel the need.

For the puff pastry crisps

1. Cut the puff pastry into 5mm slices and role out very thinly using granulated sugar instead of flour.
2. Place the strips of sugary puff pastry on a sheet of baking parchment on an oven tray. Bake at 170°C until golden.
3. Remove from the oven and cool. The strips should be very crisp.

For the caramel syrup

1. Heat the sugar in a dry pan until it reaches the caramel stage then carefully pour in half of the water.
2. The mixture will splutter and spit at first and then combine to a thick syrup. Add enough of the remaining water to give a syrup with the consistency of warm treacle. Reserve at room temperature.

To finish and serve

1. Whisk the vanilla seeds into the crème fraîche.
2. Spoon some of the apple compote into the bottom of each glass and top with the vanilla crème fraîche. Spoon a little caramel syrup over the crème fraîche then finish with a scoop of vanilla ice-cream.
3. The puff pastry crisps can be served separately or inside the glass.

Ingredients

Caramelised apple compote

1 small Bramley apple or ½ a large one, peeled and cored

4 dessert apples (Cox's, Orange Pippin, Braeburn or similar), peeled and cored

200g caster sugar

100ml water

50ml calvados, optional

Puff pastry crisps

100g bought all butter puff pastry block

3-4 tbsp granulated sugar

For the caramel syrup

125g caster sugar

125-75g water

To finish

4 heaped tbsp crème fraîche

Seeds scraped from ½ vanilla pod

Vanilla ice-cream (See Essential Basics section)

White Chocolate Truffles with Rum and Vanilla

Ingredients

100g whipping cream
1 vanilla pod, split lengthways
20g honey
25g unsalted butter
275g white chocolate
Dash of rum
300g white chocolate to coat,
optional

Method

1. Boil the whipping cream with the vanilla pod and honey, allow to infuse for 5 minutes.

2. Melt the chocolate on a medium setting in the microwave.

3. Remove the vanilla pod from the warm cream and pour into the chocolate a little at a time, mixing vigorously as you do. When all the cream is combined, you should have a smooth shiny mixture.

4. Pour the mixture into a container. Cover and refrigerate overnight.

5. The next day, scoop the truffles from the mixture using a melon baller, which has been warmed slightly over a low gas flame.

6. Chill the truffles in the fridge.

7. To finish the truffles, coat them in melted white chocolate to give a nice snappy texture to the outside when set, or for a simpler option roll them in grated white chocolate just before serving.

Simpsons

by Andreas Antona

L'École de Cuisine

Cookery School

It went so quiet in the kitchen that you could hear, well...an egg crack. There I was, in the middle of demonstrating a dish to an attentive audience at our regular cookery school experience days, when events took an unexpected turn.

Talking through the preparation as I whisked and blended, I picked up an egg and cracked it into a bowl one-handed. It's not a party trick. It's just something I learned to do when the other hand was busy stirring something else. I looked up to see mouths open in astonishment.

After the momentary silence came the clamour for an encore. "Show us how you do that" they demanded.

And so it was that 30 minutes and many boxes of eggs later, we had a roomful of people delighted with their new-found skill – and the makings of an omelette the size of the Bullring.

It's not something that happens every day, but it underlines our philosophy about cooking the Simpsons' way. Those attending that day arrived as nervous home cooks, and left a band of enthusiasts. And enthusiasm is what it's all about.

We too enjoy our regular days at the cookery school, which give visitors the chance to meet our chefs and have a look behind the scenes, followed by some hands-on experience, Champagne aperitif and three-course lunch.

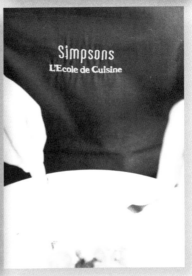

Participants in the cookery school enjoy the fruits of their labours

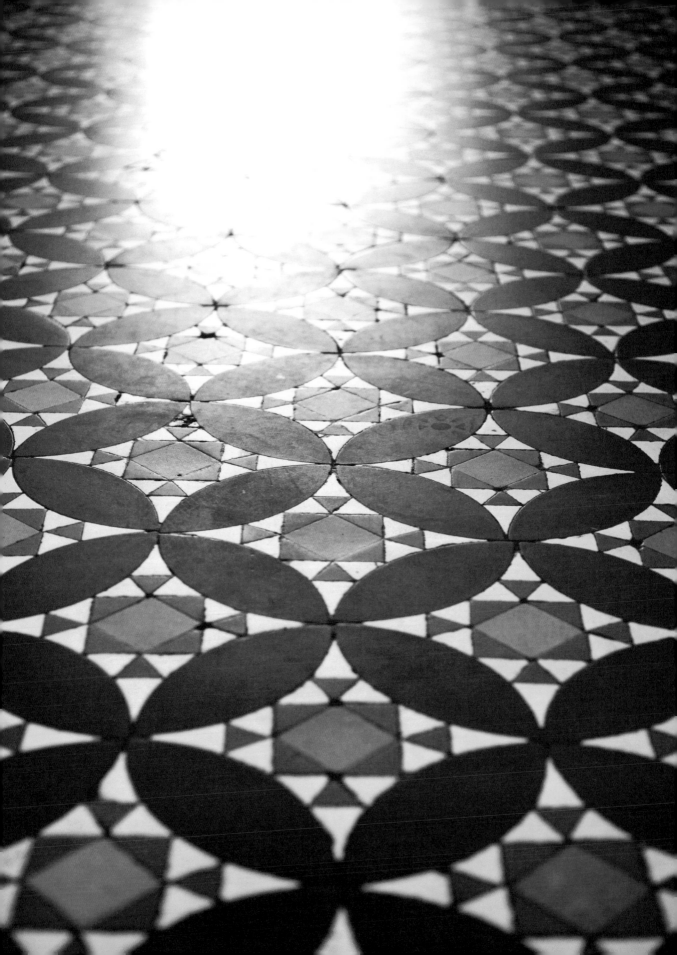

Upstairs at Simpsons

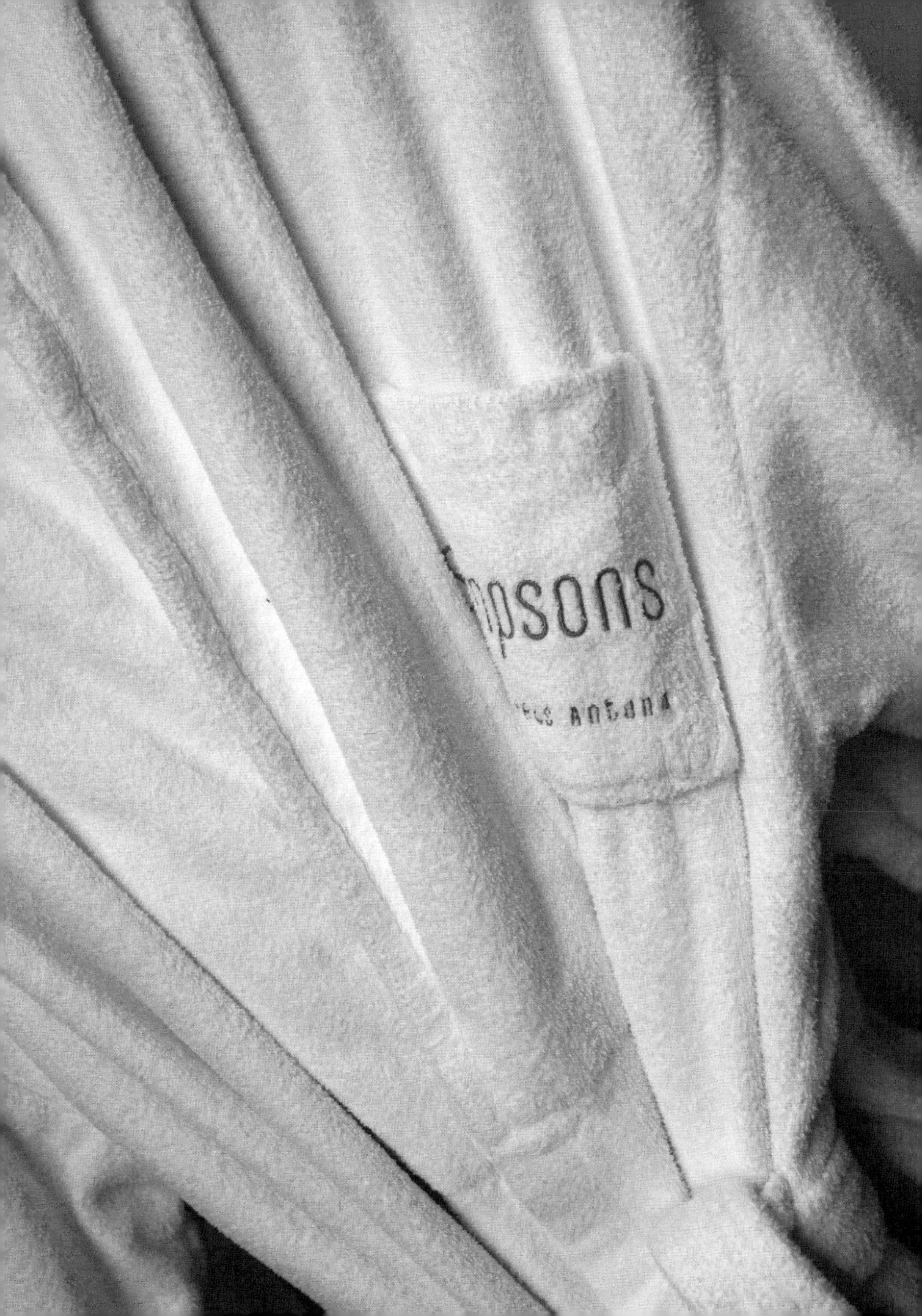

Essential Basics

Your quick guide to the simple, but oh so important bits you need to know.

Braised Ox Cheek Ravioli	Marinated Cherry Tomatoes	Slow-cooked Lamb Shoulder
Chicken Stock	Mayonnaise	Spicy Peanuts
Chickpeas	Parsley Purée	Strawberry or Raspberry Syrup
Chips	Pasta Dough	Sweet Pastry
Citrus Butter Sauce with Basil	Pig's Head Terrine	Tapenade
Crab Jus	Polenta Chips	Tempura Batter
Fennel Compote	Pomme Purée/Mashed Potato	Truffled Chicken Jus
Fish Stock	Port Sauce	Vanilla Ice-Cream
Fried Parsley Leaves	Raspberry Coulis	Vegetable Stock
Gallette Potatoes	Red Wine Sauce	Veal stock/Veal Demi-Glace
Garlic Confit	Sauce Epice	Classic/Olive Oil/Creamy Lemon vinaigrette
Globe Artichokes	Snails	
Madeira Sauce	Semi-Dried Confit Tomatoes	

Braised Ox Cheek Ravioli   Serves 4

1. Sauté the spinach with the olive oil and garlic. Drain well and chop finely.
2. Chop the cooked beef down to a coarse texture then mix well with the spinach, cheeses, herbs and egg yolk. Season with plenty of black pepper, a little salt and nutmeg.
3. Use straight away or chill until required.

For the ravioli

1. Divide the pasta into 2 pieces.
2. Roll the pasta dough out very thinly, preferably using a pasta machine.
3. If handling the pasta proves difficult, dust lightly with flour – but only if necessary.
4. Trim pasta with a knife to give 2 long strips about 40cm long and 5cm wide. Dust with semolina to prevent sticking.
5. Roll the chilled filling into balls about the size of a hazelnut.
6. Place the balls of filling along the centre of the strip, allowing 3cm space between each then brush the pasta with beaten egg.
7. Fold the pasta over the filling – take each side in turn. Press firmly between each ball of filling to seal the ravioli.
8. Next cut through the pasta between each ball of filling to give individual ravioli.
9. Store on a plate or tray dusted with semolina, cover with cling film and place in the fridge.

For the filling

100g cooked braised ox cheek

15g parmesan grated

15g ricotta cheese

1 egg yolk

1 tsp chopped parsley

1 tsp chopped marjoram

50g washed baby spinach

½ clove garlic (chopped)

1 tbsp olive oil

Salt and ground black pepper and a pinch of grated nutmeg

For the ravioli

150g fresh pasta dough (See Essential Basics section)

100g braised ox cheek ravioli filling

1 egg beaten

3 tbsp semolina for dusting

A little plain flour if necessary

Chicken Stock

Makes 1 litre

1. Put the chicken or carcasses in a saucepan and cover with 2.5 litres cold water. Bring to the boil over high heat, then immediately lower the heat and keep at a simmer.
2. After 5 minutes, skim the surface using a slotted spoon then add all the other ingredients. Cook gently for 1 hour 30 minutes, without boiling and skimming every half hour or as necessary, until you have about 1 litre.
3. Strain the stock through a wire-mesh conical sieve, which can be lined with a wet muslin cloth, and cool it as quickly as possible.

1 chicken, ideally a boiling fowl, weighing 1.5kg, or an equal weight of fresh chicken carcasses or wings

2 medium carrots, cut into chunks

White part of 2 leeks, cut into chunks

1 celery stalk, coarsely chopped

1 onion

150g button mushrooms, thinly sliced

1 bouquet garni, a large bay leaf, thyme sprig, rosemary sprig and some parsley stalks tied together

1 tsp white peppercorns

To cook Chickpeas

1. Soak the chickpeas overnight in double their volume of water.
2. Drain the chickpeas and rinse in fresh water.
3. Combine all the ingredients in a large pan and add double the volume of water to chickpeas.
4. Simmer, skimming occasionally until the chickpeas are tender. The cooking time can vary a lot depending on the quality and size of the chickpeas but around 2 hours is usually sufficient.
5. When cooked, season with salt and store the chickpeas in the cooking liquor until needed.

200g dried chickpeas

1 carrot peeled

½ onion peeled

1 stick celery

1 sprig of thyme

1 bay leaf

1 clove garlic, peeled

For the Chips

1. Peel and wash the potatoes, cut them into large chips about 1cm square, wash the chips well in cold water then plunge them into boiling, salted water. Reduce the heat immediately to a gentle simmer. Boiling too fast will cause the chips to break up before they are cooked.
2. The chips will take about 10 minutes to cook through and should be tender to the point of a knife. When ready, lift the chips from the pan with a slotted spoon, draining well and allow to cool and dry on a tray.
3. Heat your chosen oil or fat to 130°C and lower your chips into it. Cook for 5-8 minutes but remove them before they brown. Reserve on the tray until needed.

Note: Don't worry if your chips split or crack a little. This will give them a fantastic crunch.

4-6 large Maris Piper potatoes (depending on your appetite)

1 litre of duck fat, beef dripping or vegetable oil

Citrus Butter Sauce with Basil   Makes 250ml

1. Boil the orange and grapefruit juices with the shallot and reduce by half then add the cream and reduce by half again. Lower the heat and gradually whisk in the diced butter, each time allowing it to thoroughly combine with the sauce before adding more until all the butter is used.
2. Add a few drops each of orange and lemon juice to freshen the sauce, then a pinch of salt and a little sugar. Finally tear the basil into the warm sauce and infuse for 10 minutes before straining through a fine sieve. Serve immediately.

100ml freshly squeezed orange juice
40ml pink grapefruit juice
1 tsp chopped shallot
50ml double cream
200g unsalted butter, cut into small cubes
A squeeze of lemon juice
A squeeze of orange juice
A pinch of salt
A pinch of sugar
3 sprigs of basil

Crab Jus

1. Crush the crab shells with a rolling pin or meat bat. Heat the oil in a large saucepan and fry the shells over a high heat until lightly coloured.
2. Add the onion and red peppers and continue to cook vigorously for 5 minutes, then add the tomatoes and cook for a further 10 minutes.
3. Add the basil and Parma ham, if using, and cover with about 2 litres of cold water or chicken stock. Bring to the boil then lower the heat and simmer gently, uncovered, for 1 hour. Strain through a sieve, ideally lined with wet muslin, cool and chill.
4. Use as required or freeze in a 500ml block.
5. To make the stock into a crab jus simply reduce 500ml of the stock down by three quarters, then stir in 50ml of double cream and 50g of butter.

Note: You can substitute lobster for the crab shells.

400g crab shells
3 tbsp olive oil
1 small onion, chopped
2 red peppers, cored and chopped
5 tomatoes, chopped
1 sprig of fresh basil
A few Parma ham trimmings (optional)

Fennel Compote

1. Peel and de-seed the plum tomato as described for confit tomatoes on page 221. Cut the tomato flesh into 5mm cubes.
2. Wrap the thyme and star anise in muslin and tie with string.
3. Sauté the shallot and garlic in the olive oil until soft then add the fennel, a pinch of salt and the thyme and star anise bag.
4. Cook gently until the fennel has wilted then increase the heat a little to slowly caramelise the mixture.
5. After 8-10 minutes add enough chicken stock to cover and simmer gently for a further 15 minutes. Add more stock as and when required. When cooked the fennel should be completely soft with a coarse texture.

1 large head of fennel, finely sliced across the grain
1 shallot, peeled and sliced
1 plum tomato
½ tsp chopped garlic
1 sprig of thyme
1 star anise (broken up a little)
750ml chicken stock (or vegetable stock)
3 tbsp olive oil
Salt and ground white pepper

Fish Stock

Makes 1 litre

1. White fish trimmings make the best stock. Ask your fishmonger for the bones of soles, brill, turbot or whiting. If using fish heads, then remove the eyes with a thin pointed knife and the gills with kitchen scissors. Don't be tempted to use any fish skin or bones from oily fish, including salmon.
2. Rinse the fish bones and trimmings under cold running water then drain.
3. In a large saucepan, melt the butter and sweat the vegetables over low heat for a few minutes. Add the fish bones and trimmings, sauté gently for a few moments, then pour in the wine.
4. Cook until reduced by two-thirds, then add 2.5 litres cold water. Bring to the boil, lower the heat, skim the surface with a slotted spoon and add the bouquet garni, lemon slices, garlic and peppercorns. Simmer very gently for 20 minutes, skimming as necessary. Turn off the heat and leave to infuse a further 10 minutes. Gently ladle the stock through a fine-mesh conical sieve and cool it as quickly as possible.

1.5kg bones and trimmings of white fish (e.g. sole, turbot, brill, whiting) in roughly chopped pieces
50g butter
White of 2 leeks, thinly sliced
½ medium onion, thinly sliced
75g button mushrooms, thinly sliced
200ml dry white wine
1 bouquet garni
2 slices of lemon
1 glove garlic
8 white peppercorns

Fried Parsley Leaves

Simply fry leaves of flat parsley in sunflower oil at 160°C until crisp, drain well on kitchen towel and sprinkle very lightly with fine salt.

Gallette Potatoes

1. Peel the potato and cut into thin slices then use a 3.5cm cutter to cut discs from the slices.
2. Place a 10cm metal ring onto a square of baking parchment. Overlap the slices along the inner edge of the ring all the way around and place a single slice at the centre. Brush with the melted ghee and set in the fridge.
3. To cook the gallette, place it butter side down in a hot non-stick pan still inside the metal ring. Turn and crisp on both sides, season with salt and serve.

1 Maris Piper potato
6 tbsp ghee (melted)
salt

Garlic Confit

1. Separate the cloves from the stem. Prick each clove once with a cocktail stick to prevent them bursting but do not peel them.
2. Place in a saucepan and cover with the oil, ensuring the cloves are submerged. Add the herbs.
3. Cook on a very low heat, stirring occasionally until the cloves feel soft when pressed (about 30 minutes), then remove from the heat and cool in the oil. The garlic can be popped from the skin or served whole.

Use olive oil to make the confit when accompanying with fish dishes or general use, and duck fat for meat dishes
2 heads garlic with large cloves, ideally rose-skinned
About 200ml olive oil or duck fat
2 sprigs fresh thyme
1 bay leaf

To cook Globe Artichokes

1. Sweat the vegetables and herbs in the olive oil until soft. Add the white wine and reduce by half. Add the vegetable stock or water and salt. Simmer for 10 minutes.
2. Meanwhile, trim the artichokes down to the cup-shaped heart, being careful to remove all of the choke and green skin.
3. Add the artichoke hearts to the simmering stock with a pinch of salt.
4. Cover the pan and simmer until just tender to the point of a knife.
5. Cool and store in the liquid.

Note: Use the same method to cook baby artichokes also.

2 large globe artichokes

1 tbsp each of chopped carrot, celery, leek and onions

1 clove garlic, cracked

1 sprig of thyme and 1 bay leaf

75ml white wine

2 tsp lemon juice

3 tbsp olive oil

1 litre vegetable stock or water

Madeira Sauce

Makes about 200ml

Note: It is worth buying a bottle of Madeira just to make this sauce. It is surprisingly versatile.

1. Sauté the shallot and garlic in half the butter until softened.
2. Add the Madeira then boil until reduced by three quarters.
3. Pour in the demi-glace and boil until reduced by half and the liquid is nice and glossy.
4. Whisk in the remaining butter and strain to discard the shallots. Check the seasoning.

1 large shallot, chopped finely

1 clove garlic, cracked

50g butter

120ml Madeira

250ml veal demi-glace

Marinated Cherry Tomatoes

1. Bring a pan of water to the boil and be ready with a bowl of iced water.
2. Blanch the tomatoes for 2-3 seconds then transfer quickly to the iced water.
3. When cool the skins of the tomatoes will slip off easily. Put the peeled tomatoes to one side while you prepare the marinade.
4. Heat the honey until it foams up in the pan then add all of the other ingredients except the olive oil.
5. Cook for 1 minute more then add the tomatoes and remove from the heat immediately.
6. Place the tomatoes into a container and add the olive oil. Seal and leave to marinate in the fridge for 12 hours.

15 cherry tomatoes

5 coriander seeds

1 sprig rosemary

1 clove garlic, peeled and split in half

3cm piece of vanilla pod, split and seeds scraped

125g honey

10ml sherry vinegar

1 tbsp olive oil

Mayonnaise

Serves 4-6

1. Whisk the yolks, mustard, vinegar or lemon juice in a large bowl with a balloon whisk until pale and thick.
2. Gradually whisk in the oil, starting with small drops and only adding more as each lot is absorbed. If it becomes too thick then add a tablespoon of warm water to loosen it a little.
3. When all the oil is incorporated, check the seasoning and add more lemon juice if liked.
4. Chill until required.

2 free-range egg yolks
1 tsp light Dijon mustard
1 tbsp white wine vinegar or fresh lemon juice plus extra to taste
250ml groundnut or sunflower oil
Sea salt and freshly ground white pepper

Parsley Purée

1. Pick all the leaves from the parsley to give 2 good handfuls.
2. Drop the leaves into boiling salted water and boil very fast for about a minute or until tender, drain the leaves and plunge into iced water for 30 seconds and drain again.
3. Purée in a liquidiser with a little water and a tablespoon or so of olive oil.
4. Pass the purée through a fine sieve and season to taste with salt.

1 large bunch of flat leaf parsley
Salt
Olive oil

Pasta Dough

Makes about 800g

Note: It is best to make a full quantity of this recipe as you will find it much easier to handle a larger amount of dough. Leftover dough freezes well either in a ball or cut into noodles.

1. Place all the ingredients into a food processor and pulse until they form into clumps. Turn out onto a worktop and knead with your hands to a smooth dough that is firm not sticky.
2. Wrap in cling film and rest for an hour or so. Divide the dough into 8 and roll each piece on a lightly-floured worktop into 3mm thick rectangles (the thickness of a 1 pound coin).
3. Feed each rectangle through a pasta machine several times starting with the thickest setting and finishing with the thinnest.
4. The pasta is now ready for use. For filled shapes, e.g. tortellini, use the pasta just rolled; for cutting into noodles etc. allow the sheets to dry slightly so they cut cleanly.

550g plain flour
½ tsp fine sea salt
4 medium free-range eggs
6 egg yolks
2 tbsp olive oil

Pig's Head Terrine

This terrine is used in the pork fillet dish on page 127. Half a pig's head is the minimum practical quantity. That will yield more than you need, but remember it will freeze well in handy-sized chunks.

The terrine also makes an excellent first course in its own right – coat portion-sized slabs in egg and breadcrumb, shallow fry on both sides till crisp and hot then serve with a little green salad and some tartare sauce.

A real test of your foodie credentials!

1. First shave your meat – or scorch the hairs off with a blow torch.

2. Place all of the meat in a pan large enough to accommodate it and the vegetables easily. (This will be easier if your half pigs head has been cut in half again by the butcher)

3. Cover with cold water and bring the pan to a simmer for about 10 minutes. Discard the water and resulting impurities then cover again with fresh cold water and bring to a simmer.

4. Cook for about 20 minutes, skimming off any impurities regularly. Add the vegetables, herbs and spices and vinegar.

5. Simmer very gently, skimming occasionally, until the meat is completely tender and falling from the bone – about 3-4 hours. Top up with hot water when necessary.

6. When the meat is cooked remove to a tray and allow to cool – but only just enough for it not to burn your fingers while you pick through.

7. Strain the cooking liquor into a wide pan and boil to reduce. You should be left with a small amount of sticky juice. To test it, put a spoonful on a saucer as you would when testing jam for setting. The mixture will set to a firm jelly in the fridge within about 5 minutes. You may need to transfer the liquor to a smaller pan about halfway through the process to prevent scorching at the edges.

8. While the liquor is reducing, pick through the meat. The basic principle is to get rid of any bones, gristle and blood vessels but keep as much meat, skin and fat as possible. It's a little trying for the squeamish but stick with it as the result is worthwhile.

9. Once you have a nice pile of porky morsels, shred through them with a chopping knife on a large chopping board to give a coarse texture. The ears may need special attention to make them a little finer.

10. You should now have a bowl of warm shredded pork and the liquor reduced to a jelly.

11. Season the meat with salt and pepper then add the parsley, mustard and enough of the jelly to give a porridge-type consistency.

12. Take a suitably-sized terrine dish or tray and line it with cling film. Pour in the pork mixture. It will find its own level with a light tap or 2.

13. Refrigerate the terrine for a minimum of 2 hours after which it will be firm enough to slice and use as you wish.

Half a pig's head soaked in cold water overnight

1kg piece of belly pork on the bone

2 pig's trotters

2 tsp salt

3 carrots, peeled, topped and tailed

2 onions, peeled and halved

3 sticks of celery, washed

1 leek, split and washed

A generous sprig of thyme

5 bay leaves

5 cloves

2 tsp white peppercorns

75ml white wine vinegar

4 tbsp flatleaf parsley, coarsely chopped

Grain mustard to taste

For the Polenta Chips

1. Bring the water and the salt to the boil, gradually whisk in the polenta flour to give a porridge-type consistency.
2. Reduce the heat to low and continue to stir until the polenta is cooked (about 10 minutes or as directed on the pack).
3. Remove from the heat. Beat in the parmesan and butter then pour the hot polenta into a deep plastic container and refrigerate. The polenta will set to quite a firm texture when chilled – allow about 2 hours.
4. Remove the tub of set polenta from the fridge and turn out onto a chopping board. Cut into chunky chips, roll in a little plain flour and reserve in the fridge.

575ml water
Pinch of salt
125g polenta flour (quick cook type)
65g grated parmesan
10g butter
1 litre vegetable oil for deep-frying
2 tbsp plain flour

Pomme Purée/Mashed Potato

1. Peel the potatoes and cut into even-sized pieces. Bring them to the boil in lightly-salted water and simmer until tender to the point of a knife.
2. Strain the potatoes and return them to the dry pan. Place over a low heat and shake a little for 3-4 minutes to steam away any remaining moisture (the more moisture you remove the more cream and butter you can add).
3. Remove from the heat and mash the potatoes – preferably with a ricer but a hand masher is fine if you are thorough.
4. Heat the cream or milk in a pan. Meanwhile, stir the butter into the hot potatoes then add enough of the hot cream or milk to give your preferred consistency.
5. Finally, finish with salt, pepper and grated nutmeg (optional).

Note: Different varieties of potato will absorb more or less cream and butter so add them gradually.

900g Maris Piper potatoes (or another floury variety)
160g unsalted butter
160g cream or milk
A pinch each of salt and white pepper
A grating of nutmeg

Port Sauce   Serves 4-6

1. Put the shallots, mushrooms, blackcurrants and orange zest into a saucepan and pour in the Port. Bring to the boil and cook until reduced by a half.
2. Add the veal demi-glace and simmer until reduced down by about half again, about 25 minutes. Skim the surface with a slotted spoon if any scum forms.
3. Add the cream and boil for 3 minutes. Check the seasoning and serve.

50g chopped shallots
100g chopped mushrooms
50g fresh or frozen blackcurrants
1 small strip orange zest
200ml ruby Port
300ml veal demi-glace
3 tbsp double cream
Sea salt and freshly ground black pepper

Raspberry Coulis

1. Purée the raspberries, sugar and lemon juice in a liquidiser. Pass through a fine sieve.

300g fresh or good quality frozen raspberries

100g caster sugar

Squeeze of lemon

Red Wine Sauce

1. Sauté the shallots, mushrooms and garlic until beginning to colour. Add in the red wine and reduce by two thirds then add the veal jus and thyme.
2. Simmer, skimming occasionally until reduced to a coating consistency. Strain the sauce into another pan, whisk in the butter and serve.

Note: Perfect and very adaptable, it can be served with beef, veal, chicken and game dishes. Try substituting one third of the veal jus with fish stock to give a robust fish sauce.

50g sliced button mushrooms

50g sliced shallots

1 garlic clove, cracked

Pinch of cracked white peppercorns

200ml full bodied red wine

300ml veal jus

1 sprig fresh thyme

50g diced butter

Sauce Epice

1. Put all the ingredients into a saucepan, bring to the boil then simmer until reduced to a syrupy consistency that will cover the back of a spoon, about 150ml. Check seasoning, strain and set aside.

250ml red wine vinegar

200g soft brown sugar

3 star anise

1 tsp coriander seeds

1 tbsp dried pink peppercorns, optional

1 tsp fennel seeds

Sea salt and freshly ground black pepper

For the Snails

1. Drain the rinsed snails. In a medium saucepan, combine the chicken stock, vegetables, garlic, herbs and wine. Simmer for 15 minutes then add the snails, a good pinch of salt and a lid. Cook the snails very gently for around an 1½ hours or until very tender. Cool and reserve in the cooking liqueur.

Note: The snails can be used straight from the jar after a good rinse in cold water but can be a little chewy. If you like your snails tender then cook them as above.

1 small jar of large cooked snails (soaked in cold water overnight)

1 tbsp each of finely chopped onion, carrot, leek and celery

2 cloves garlic, cracked

Sprig of thyme

Bay leaf

1 glass white wine

500ml chicken stock or water (See Essential Basics section)

75g butter

½ tsp chopped garlic

Semi-Dried Confit Tomatoes

1. Blanch the tomatoes in a large pan of boiling water for just 6 seconds then plunge into a bowl of iced water for a minute. Drain, peel, halve and scoop out the seeds, then pat dry with paper towel.
2. Heat an oven to the lowest setting. Lay out the tomatoes cut side up in a tray. Dot with the garlic slices, scatter over the thyme leaves, then the oil, salt and sugar.
3. Bake for up to 2 hours until the flesh shrinks back a little and feels tender. Remove and cool. Store in a fridge until required.

10 ripe plum tomatoes
2 cloves garlic, sliced thinly
10 sprigs fresh thyme, leaves only
2 tbsp olive oil
1 tsp sea salt
1 tsp caster sugar

Slow-cooked Lamb Shoulder

1. Season the lamb well with salt. Heat the fat with the garlic and thyme then add the lamb.
2. Simmer very gently for about 20 minutes then cover the pan and cook in the oven at 90°C for around 4 hours or until completely tender.
3. Remove from the oven and lift the lamb out of the fat. Pick through the meat, which should break apart easily, discarding any fat and sinew. When you have all the meat together shred it into a bowl. Take the 2 cooked garlic cloves and squeeze out the purée into the lamb. Season with black pepper and salt then mix in a little of the duck fat – use just enough to moisten and bind.
4. Line a suitably-sized container with cling film, press the mixture in and wrap well.
5. Place in the fridge and put something heavy on top to press the mixture as it chills. Leave overnight to set.

1kg piece of lamb shoulder, boned out
2 cloves of garlic
A sprig of thyme
Enough duck or goose fat to cover the lamb in a snugly-fitting pan

Spicy Peanuts

1. Place the sugar, salt, cayenne and water in a pan and boil to dissolve, cook until the mixture becomes a little syrupy – about a minute or so.
2. Add the nuts to the pan and stir to coat. Tip onto a baking tray lined with parchment paper.
3. Bake at 175°C until golden for around 8-12 minutes. Remove from the oven and cool on the tray. Store in an airtight container to keep crisp.

Note: We use these spicy peanuts with the beef dish on page 154, but they are best as a nibble with drinks or crushed and sprinkled over salads. Experiment with other types of nut – almonds or cashews for example.

125g peeled peanuts
25g sugar
10g salt
10g cayenne pepper
90g water

Strawberry or Raspberry Syrup

1. Place all the ingredients in a heatproof bowl.
2. Place the bowl over a pan of simmering water for 30-45 minutes, stirring occasionally.
3. Strain the mixture gently through a fine sieve or muslin. Reserve the syrup in the fridge until needed and discard the berries.

500g ripe strawberries or raspberries, washed, hulled and sliced

50g caster sugar

2 tsp lemon juice

Sweet Pastry

1. Place the flour, butter, sugar and salt in a mixing bowl and rub together with your fingers until you have the texture of fresh breadcrumbs.
2. Beat together the whole egg and egg yolk in a separate bowl then add the egg to the flour mixture and stir to combine.
3. Do not overwork the mixture but do ensure it is mixed properly. Wrap the finished pastry in cling film and refrigerate until set enough to roll (about 2 hours).

225g plain flour

150g unsalted butter

75g icing sugar

A pinch of salt

1 egg

1 egg yolk

Tapenade

200g pitted black olives

75ml olive oil

15g capers

2 anchovy fillets

1 tsp lemon juice

½ tsp chopped garlic

1. Place all the ingredients in a blender and blend to a smooth paste. Rub through a fine sieve with the back of a ladle.

Tempura Batter

1 egg yolk

150ml ice-cold sparkling mineral water

100g plain flour

1. Quickly whisk together the egg yolk and water then tip in the flour all at once and whisk until just combined and the consistency of double cream. Do not over-whisk.

Truffled Chicken Jus

1. Coat the chopped chicken wings with the vegetable oil and roast in a heavy roasting tray at 200°C until golden. Turn the wings over once or twice during cooking. When thoroughly roasted, drain off any excess oil and add the garlic and shallots to the tray. Return to the oven for 5 minutes or so to soften the shallots a little.

2. Place the tray over a medium heat and pour in the white wine and reduce by two thirds. Tip the contents of the tray into a suitably-sized saucepan and add half the chicken stock. Then bring to the boil and skim any froth or grease from the surface. Add the thyme and peppercorns. Simmer until reduced by half then add the remaining chicken stock.

3. Simmer to reduce again, skimming occasionally until the sauce becomes a little syrupy and has a good chicken flavour. At this point strain the sauce through a fine sieve into a clean pan and if necessary reduce a little more.

4. When you are happy with the consistency, whisk in the butter followed by the truffle oil and/or the chopped truffle if you have it. Add a tiny squeeze of lemon juice just to balance the richness of the butter. Serve.

Note: Thin with a little chicken stock and use a hand blender to create a truffle foam. This sauce is great with chicken but also firm textured fish like turbot or Dover sole.

800g chopped chicken wings or carcass
75ml vegetable oil
4 shallots, peeled and finely sliced
4 garlic cloves cracked
150ml dry white wine
1.5 litres of chicken stock
75g butter
1 sprig of thyme
10 white peppercorns
A few drops of truffle oil
2 tsp finely chopped truffle
A squeeze of lemon juice

Vanilla Ice-Cream

1. Bring the milk, cream and vanilla to the boil.

2. Meanwhile, lightly whisk together the yolks and sugar.

3. Whisk the hot milk and cream into the yolks then return the mixture to the pan over a low heat.

4. Cook gently, stirring constantly, until the mixture has thickened enough to coat the back of a spoon.

5. Pass the mixture through a fine sieve into a bowl and cool down before churning in an ice-cream machine.

6. Reserve in the freezer when ready.

2 vanilla pods, split and scraped
450ml milk
150ml double cream
6 egg yolks
120g caster sugar

Vegetable Stock

Makes 1 Litre

1. Put all the ingredients in a saucepan. Add 2 litres of cold water. Bring to the boil over high heat, then cook at a bare simmer for 35 minutes, skimming as necessary until reduced by half and you have around 1 litre of liquid.

2. Strain through a fine-mesh conical sieve into a bowl and cool as quickly as possible.

3 medium carrots, cut into rounds
White part of 2 leeks, thinly sliced
2 celery sticks, thinly sliced
¼ bulb fennel, very thinly sliced
3 shallots, thinly sliced
1 medium onion, thinly sliced
2 unpeeled garlic cloves
1 bouquet garni – a large bay leaf, thyme sprig, rosemary sprig and some parsley stalks tied together
250ml dry white wine
10 white peppercorns, crushed

Veal stock/Veal Demi-Glace

2kg veal bones, chopped
½ pig's trotter
1 large carrot
1 small onion
2 sticks celery
4 cloves garlic, cracked
4 tbsp sunflower oil
200ml white wine
400g ripe tomatoes, chopped
200g button mushrooms, sliced
1 sprig of thyme
2 bay leaves
Few parsley stalks
1 tsp of white peppercorns

1. Roast the bones and trotter at 200°C. Turn once during the cooking until well browned.
2. Meanwhile sauté the onion, celery, carrot and garlic in the base of a large stockpot until lightly coloured then add the tomatoes and mushrooms. Cook for 5 minutes more. Add the white wine and reduce by two thirds.
3. Add the roasted bones and trotter to the pan and cover with cold water. Bring to the boil and skim thoroughly, then add the herbs and peppercorns. Cook gently for 6 hours, skimming and topping up with water occasionally.
4. Pass the stock through muslin-lined sieve and cool.

For the Veal demi-glace:

1. Simply boil the finished veal stock to reduce it by half. This gives a richer version of the veal stock – convenient when making brown sauces quickly.

Classic/Olive Oil/Creamy Lemon Vinaigrette

Serves 4

For the classic vinaigrette

1 tsp Dijon mustard
Juice of 1 lemon
90ml groundnut oil
Sea salt and freshly ground black pepper

For the classic vinaigrette

1. In a bowl, whisk together the mustard and lemon juice adding salt and pepper to taste.
2. Whisk in the oil and use as soon as possible. If it starts to separate out, whisk again.

Olive Oil Vinaigrette

50ml white wine vinegar
250ml extra virgin olive oil
Pinch salt
Smaller pinch sugar
Squeeze of lemon juice

For the olive oil vinaigrette

1. Simply whisk everything together in a bowl or shake together in a bottle or a screwtop jar.
2. Shake or whisk well before use.
3. Note – this will keep for several weeks in the fridge.

Creamy Lemon Vinaigrette

3 egg yolks
300ml grapeseed oil
2 tbsp lemon juice
1 tsp sugar
Grain mustard
Dijon mustard
Pinch salt
Pinch white pepper
1 tbsp chopped mixed herbs (optional)

For the creamy lemon vinaigrette

1. Combine the egg yolks with everything except the grapeseed oil and the herbs (if using) in a bowl.
2. Whisk to combine then gradually whisk in the grapeseed oil to form a creamy emulsion.
3. You should aim for a consistency similar to double cream – adjust with water if necessary.

Note: This can be kept for up to 1 week in the fridge.